CHILDREN IN HOMES

by

KENNETH BRILL

and

RUTH THOMAS

LONDON
VICTOR GOLLANCZ LTD
1965

First published August 1964
Second impression February 1965

Printed in Great Britain by
The Camelot Press Ltd., London and Southampton

PREFACE

THE EXPERIENCE OF children's committees, extending over more than sixteen years, provides material for a review of some of the salient features of care for children in residential establishments. In 1946 such children were variously described as "deprived" and "homeless" and a memorandum of evidence submitted to the Curtis Committee and subsequently published[1] bore the title *Children without Homes*. This book was widely read, both by the staffs who were transferred from Public Assistance and Education Committees and by the new corps of professionally trained workers who have come into the Children's Service of local authorities and voluntary societies. The late Dame Evelyn Fox in her Foreword to *Children without Homes* said:

> "This may be the beginning of a new venture of outstanding significance and it is hoped that the present publication, based as it is on the long experience of specially trained workers, may serve as a useful handbook for those who will be the first trainees under the new Scheme. Their pioneer work will have far-reaching consequences in raising the standards of institutional care throughout the country and it should result, in the course of the next few years, in making this account of conditions prevailing in 1946 hopelessly outdated and of interest only as a measure of the progress which has ensued."

In many respects Dame Evelyn's prediction has come true; in other respects progress has been slow. Any account of conditions in 1946 is now hopelessly out-dated and we can no longer fairly describe children in residential care as being without homes. But the basic needs of childhood remain the same.

It is now many years since it was first generally recognised that one of the surest ways of raising the standard of citizenship lay in affording a universally high standard of education to all children and young people. Side by side with the continuous movement to improve education for youth have gone parallel efforts to raise standards of health. In 1963 an even more fundamental move to raise the conditions of family life in

---

[1] *Children without Homes* by Ruth Thomas, pub. National Association for Mental Health.

which children are reared was made by the Children and Young Persons Act. This last move was so clearly essential to the success of our health and education schemes that only in a topsy-turvy world would it have emerged so belatedly in a social programme.

Teachers, nurses and doctors dealing with children have always realised that the furtherance of their best endeavours was dependent on the quality of understanding and social standards in the child's home. By this they have meant not only that good parents co-operated and prevented the State's educational efforts becoming abortive, but that, where family background is bad, social services become a constant patching of a garment being as constantly torn.

The programme (which is now well on the way to achievement), first to ensure a sound economic basis for family life and adequate material conditions, and then to provide comprehensive health and education services, guards the boundaries of family life. Most families are able to keep the management of their difficulties in their own hands, but there remain those few who, through death, illness or deviations of personality, are unable to care properly for their children. It is no accident that the generation which has set itself the task of ensuring good conditions for family life has also taken up in earnest the condition of the child away from his parents.

Since 1948 there has been an enormous development in the services designed to keep the child at home, by improved health visiting, education welfare and N.S.P.C.C. work, by help in family budgeting, by home helps and sensitive housing management and by the preventive casework services of family service units, child-guidance clinics and public health and children's departments. The first emphasis is on prevention. If that fails, the second is on modifying the home so that the child can be restored. The next line of defence is the substitute home, provided by fostering or adoption. This fourfold attack, prevention, restoration, fostering and adoption, occupies the greater part of the energies of the children's services, leaving fewer children in residential care than there were a decade ago. Of those in residential Homes, fewer think of themselves as being without parents or families, since more strenuous efforts are made to keep them in touch.

This book is about the child in residential care in Homes and Nurseries and the like. On the surface he is already given education and health services as good as those provided for more fortunate children in their own homes. His material well-being is in many respects protected and sometimes over-protected. But the anomalies of his position are patent, and the dividends which health and school education pay in liberating his social effectiveness and his capacity to enjoy life are so clearly insufficient that special thought and effort are needed to compensate him for the loss of ordinary family life.

While we have attempted to cover the problems of children in residential care from a number of angles that seem important to us, there is one group of children about whom we have said nothing. We distinguish between the normal child living apart from his family, who may sometimes be classed as a difficult child and sometimes as very difficult, and a further group who (whether living at home or in care) may be technically classed as *delinquent*.

A child under the age of eleven can rarely be assigned to this group, since short-lived periods of social intransigence are to be expected up to this age. They do not necessarily indicate that a compulsively anti-social character is developing, though they may well do so. Our knowledge is at present inadequate to enable us to make a prognosis in any individual case. On the other hand signs of delinquency may appear for the first time just prior to or during adolescence without earlier marked signs of instability.

Lawyers may see delinquency as a single problem, their attention being directed mainly to its behavioural aspects. But the psychologist is aware that the delinquent group contains personalities of very diverse origin and structure, whose intractable behaviour may spring from a wide variety of motives. While much that is said about children in this book applies equally to the delinquent child, simply because he is a child, some of it is not applicable to him. Delinquency cannot for the most part be resolved by good mothering or fathering, though it may be true that some kinds of delinquent character might not have developed had parental care been adequate.

Those with the onerous task of managing delinquent children in residential care require a special training and psychiatric guidance to enable them to differentiate between diverse types requiring radically different handling. An approach which is adequate and helpful for one type may be disastrous for another, and for some problems of delinquency psychiatric guidance is still woefully at a loss. This is not to say, however, that it is bankrupt. To discuss the care of delinquent children would require a separate memorandum in which methods of care and handling could be considered in relation to the various personality structures of different types of delinquent. But so long as a background of specialist training and guidance for those who undertake this work is lacking such a memorandum by itself could not fail to be misleading.

What follows is not intended to be an exhaustive survey of the field of residential care: it is selective, like the experience of the writers. Both have worked in the field of residential child care. Ruth Thomas' practical experience was gained in the wartime scheme for evacuated children, in hostels for maladjusted children and in the Home for maladjusted infants and older children run by the National Association for Mental Health on behalf of the Ministry of Health during, and immediately after, the war. Since shortly after the publication of the Curtis Report she has been practising as a psycho-analyst. Kenneth Brill was appointed children's officer for a county borough in 1948 when the new service was set up and has, for the past twelve years, been children's officer for a rural county. His experience is based upon discussion with the staff of residential Homes and with child care workers serving the voluntary Homes as well as other local authorities.

We have attempted to pool our resources and direct them to those problems which seem uppermost at present in the minds of child care workers, hoping that, as Dame Evelyn Fox foresaw seventeen years ago, these problems will in turn become out-dated. This can, of course, only lead to the high-lighting of more and more opportunities for forward movement, to which there is no end in the complex business of bringing up children in groups away from their parents.

For help in the preparation of this book we acknowledge our indebtedness to many colleagues, and particularly to Miss Mary Joynson, A.A.P.S.W., Miss Olive Stevenson, M.A., and Mrs. Marianne Pincombe, and to the Regional Representatives of the National Association for Mental Health who provided many of the examples which have been quoted from *Children without Homes*.

KENNETH BRILL

March, 1964. RUTH THOMAS

CONTENTS

Part One

THE NEEDS OF CHILDHOOD

Part Two

VARIETIES OF RESIDENTIAL CARE

Part One

THE NEEDS OF CHILDHOOD

CHAPTER ONE

INTRODUCTION

WHAT CONDITIONS OF upbringing enable a child to achieve a healthy maturity? If the child is reasonably approving and adequately critical of people and conditions in his early life, this attitude will transfer itself in large part to his adult dealings and will be shown in self-assurance and a willingness to face and clear away real difficulties. If, on the other hand, he is beaten by childhood conditions, he may be either defeated in advance by adult life, or else be too tragically rebellious to see its difficulties with a sense of proportion, and so be unable to use his powers to meet them. The question overshadowing all others is this: how does the world of family, foster home or Home look to the child when he views it from the angle of his needs? In short, what does *he* find satisfactory?

It is necessary to set out in some detail an analysis of the basic needs of childhood. The emphasis throughout is on the child's view of life. This is constantly changing. Good parents are able to play a constructive part in this change, to the extent that they are closely aware of the child's needs. Indeed, the good family is so successful as an educator because it concedes so much to the child's point of view—willing affection and intimacy, for example, and continuous close personal relationships which furnish his ideals and standards. It caters for his *emotional* life and takes his peculiarities in its stride, recognising them indeed as making up his personality. It understands that a child's wishes and moods are "himself" to an extent which is unallowable in adulthood. Harassing and difficult moods and tiresome peculiarities and insistences are a necessary part of his make-up. The child is open to education only through his feelings, some of which may be unpleasant to us, and the good parent is aware that unless children's emotions are respected they may end by denying feeling altogether. If this stage of unattachment is reached, the parent is defeated, because the child is no longer accessible to influence.

There are, of course, many angles from which the needs of the child must be approached—for example, those of good material provision, hygenic living, parental rights and administrative and economic necessities. This account gives priority to the child's emotional needs as directive forces in his growth to maturity, with, it is hoped, adequate regard to the other factors.

No substitute home can in fact replace the family, and although children in foster homes sometimes have certain advantages over their fellows in residential care, basic needs cannot be fully met there either. The problem in both instances is, how can a substitute home conserve what remains of the child's own family relationships and go some way to compensate him for his loss, so that he may take his place in the community as little handicapped as possible by the artificial conditions of his upbringing?

If a child has to be away from his home, his needs can generally best be met by the intimacy and individual understanding to be found in a foster home or in a small Home which approximates to a family of boys and girls of varying ages. But there is a danger of the foster home and the so-called "family group Home" being put forward as the twin panaceas for every child whose family is, for the time being, unable to care for him. Experience shows that many children formerly described as "homeless" have in fact solid emotional and material attachments to their own families; the task then is not to provide a substitute family (which the child may well violently reject) but to provide a warm, secure and understanding environment in which he can be nurtured while his links with his family are strengthened and his relatives are helped to prepare themselves to receive him back. This calls for a wide variety of provision, including the following: Reception Homes and Reception Nurseries; Hostels and Boarding Schools for the mal-adjusted and educationally subnormal; ordinary Boarding Schools; Approved Schools; and children's Homes. None of these, however, is sufficient in itself; each is a therapeutic community which the child is helped to regard, according to his degree of understanding, as a place of temporary stay, from which he ordinarily looks forward to a return to family life. It is vital that the staff of such institutions should be outward-looking persons who are not seeking to take the place of real parents and that the family should be kept open, for each child, by a trained caseworker who is recognised by the child and resident staff and family alike as having a specific responsibility for that child.

The most important single factor in the building up of family life is the quality of affection and understanding which the parents give to each other and to the children and the way in which they interpret their responsibility as parents. It is therefore a necessity for all workers to have a knowledge of the child's needs at all stages, from birth through the whole period he is in care.

Child care workers, whether they are the administrative officers of local authorities or of voluntary societies, medical officers responsible for the physical care of the homeless child, caseworkers helping children and parents or foster parents, or the staffs of Homes in direct contact with the children, need to understand in detail how family life in normal circumstances meets the child's emotional needs. Only so equipped can workers select and supervise good foster homes, restore children to families who have been prepared to receive them, or consider how best to replace this loss in residential Homes. Only so, indeed, can workers be fitted to make the most important decision of all, the decision whether to receive the child into care for the time being or whether to leave him at home.

Some officers concerned with children have considerable technical knowledge of particular aspects of child life, for example of children's physical needs, either material or medical. But when such technical knowledge has been acquired in a form unrelated to a knowledge of children's total needs, there is no end to the errors into which such trained staff can fall when they seek to apply their technical skill to the management of children's lives. It is therefore imperative that training in these technical matters—for example, domestic, nursing and physical care, shall not be divorced from an all-round knowledge of the child as a living human being. This is why it is so necessary that a basic training in the understanding of children should form part of the equipment of all workers who deal with children.

Some of the illustrative material in this book has been selected to show that it is not advisable merely to graft new types of training in child care on to existing training, but to ensure that each is inter-penetrated by the other.

The importance of this interpenetration has been amply demonstrated by experience in children's departments. It is not a question of getting everybody some kind of training, but of ensuring that all who play a part in caring for and making decisions about children shall have a grasp of the realities and a common body of principles. Here are a few of the people whose attitudes may play a decisive part in determining the whole future life and happiness of a child: the N.S.P.C.C. inspector; the education welfare officer; the health visitor; the housing manager; the police inspector; the family doctor; the probation officer; the child guidance worker; the magistrate. When a child is in care the attitudes of the following may be equally significant: the reception home warden; the remand home superintendent; the housemother; the local authority medical officer; the child care officer; the committee member. The sixteen years since 1948 have been a period of tension in which the clash of feeling and opinion has not always operated to the benefit of the children. Some workers have been preoccupied with physical hygiene; others with administrative convenience; others with monetary economy; others with committee appraisal; others with boarding-out percentages—and a few in each group have been preoccupied with doctrinaire theories.

The spread of understanding has been helped by inter-disciplinary conferences, especially those held to discuss particular families, such as those held in reception homes and child guidance clinics and under the auspices of the co-ordinating officer appointed to investigate allegations of ill treatment and neglect. There is a risk of the individual agency getting little more than a black-and-white snapshot of the child himself at a point in time, when what is wanted is more like a coloured stereoscopic cinemascope film of the child's whole life. The colour of feelings; 3D to give perspective; a wide screen to take in the other people of importance in his life; a picture of his likely future if each of the various alternative kinds of action is taken, and a detailed study of his past life. As has been often quoted, "there is no future for a child with no past".

Perhaps the most significant development of such case conferences over the years is that they have increasingly tended in practice towards the formulation of plans which will preserve family relationships. There is a risk of the individual agency's reaching the end of its tether after a lengthy, and perhaps ill-advised, pursuit of a particular line. When all the agencies confer, it is most notable how there is nearly always a majority opinion in favour of some kind of conservative treatment. Even where removal of the children becomes inevitable there will generally be offers of help designed to ensure their ultimate restoration.

As the aim of all upbringing is to enable the child to take his place in the community, training should include a knowledge of how best to give the homeless child access to contacts with the community in which he lives and, above all, with his own family. This is equally necessary whether the child is placed in a foster home or in residential care.

In a good foster home the child automatically has access to the life of the community. But with foster parents whose attitude is not, in the best sense, parental, a child can be as poorly equipped for normal living as one brought up in the relative isolation of a Home. Means must therefore be devised to bring to people's attention their responsibilities towards the child in their midst who is living away from his parents.

Throughout this account of conditions for the care of children the following points are emphasised:

That strong links should be maintained with the child's own family, by unremitting casework designed to ensure his return; or failing that, to preserve the child's exclusive feelings towards his own people.

That children in care share the common needs of childhood for a good home and a full and happy family life.

That conditions under which such children have to live should approximate, so far as possible, materially and psychologically, to those enjoyed by children in a good family.

That only by the fullest study and understanding of children and grown-ups can those responsible hope to compensate the child in care for the loss of his family.

CHAPTER TWO

WHAT LIVING WITHOUT A FAMILY MEANS TO THE CHILD

BEFORE CONSIDERING HOW far the needs of the child for a family can be met in residential care let us look at the evidence we have from the children themselves. The evidence shows that family attachments are difficult to replace and that when these have in fact for one reason or another to be broken or interrupted, the children experience very considerable suffering. In later chapters we will return to these findings and consider how far and in what way the needs of the child as we have outlined them can to some extent be met in residential care.

Make-believe parents

The records of children in care show how keenly they feel being without family and parents and how they compensate themselves in imagination by make-believe parents.

A child of five whose parent was forbidden by the Court to see her, showed a new dress given to her by the matron and said, "My mummy sent me this; she came to see me this morning in the bathroom. You didn't know, did you?"

A worker writes: "I put Richard's pyjamas on back to front. He is aged nine. He said, 'My mummy doesn't like them that way,' and we undid them. He has no mother."

A visiting worker to a Home was asked by a child of ten: "Be my visitor: I won't stay here another visiting day without my own visitor."

Kathleen, aged three, has been in a nursery since she was a baby. Her mother is in a mental hospital and there has been no word from her for two years. Kathleen appears to be devoted to her nursery nurse. However, when she had to go to hospital she noticed that other children had mothers and fathers on visiting day. She said, "When I leave here I'm going to see my mummy." On return to the nursery her behaviour was exceptionally difficult and demanding.

It used to be commonplace in residential nurseries and children's Homes for children to approach strangers, and members of the field staff, and call them "Daddy" and "Mummy". They quarrelled over each other's visitors for the right to give them these titles.

William aged six, who was brought up in a nursery after one unsuccessful attempt at fostering, said to a Visitor, "Miss W. visits me every Saturday; my mummy and daddy have been to see me too, and they are coming again." Miss W. was the officer concerned with placing him in the foster home. It was not true that she visited him so frequently nor that he had heard from his father and mother.

Suzette, aged four, said after Christmas, "My daddy sent me these presents." She is in a nursery with other children who received presents from their fathers, but Suzette's father's whereabouts are unknown and she has never heard from him, although she is visited by her mother.

Margaret, aged ten, has been in care since birth. Her mother is severely subnormal. She has seen her mother twice in ten years. She said, "My mummy is going to get a house soon and have me to live with her."

The child's desire to talk about his absent family

At one time children with poor family histories entering Homes, brooded over memories which they had no means of sharing in the new surroundings. Their life-stories were never discussed with them; they felt no one but themselves knew about their previous lives (which was often true as far as the Home was concerned), and would have been glad of the relief of talking, to break the secrecy and isolation which surrounded them. Memory in these cases proved a barrier to forming new relationships.

One warden (children 7 to 14) was so impressed with the extent of this problem that she made a point of letting all children know soon after entry that she understood something of their history, and found this a very firm and reassuring bond with each one.

Some residential nurseries have been at great pains to keep alive the children's memories of their parents.

Miss Smith takes great trouble to know the parents and has photographs of most of them and talks to the children frequently about their fathers and mothers (children 0 to 5).

Whenever possible, there is a photograph of a parent over each child's bed and a nightly ceremony of saying good night to mum and dad (children 2 to 5).

Some nurseries are reluctant to use this device because of jealousy where some children have no parents. But one nursery overcame this difficulty by the staff having polyphotos taken, and in the end each child had, at least, someone's photograph.

The need for contact between brothers and sisters

Where several children of the same family are in a Home together it is easier to keep alive memories and cement family feeling. In former times, children of one family tended to be split up according to age and sex. It was not unusual to find a family of six children distributed over three or four widely scattered Homes. Now, as a rule, they are kept together. That some brothers and sisters do not get on with each other is rarely an adequate reason for separating them.

Piers, aged five, was committed to a nursery two years ago, in company with his two younger brothers, on account of parental neglect. He has always felt responsible for Billy and Danny and leaves no one in any doubt about the relationship. Attempts were made to get him to go away with an "Auntie" for the week-end. He went to tea and said, "I can't stay the night here because there is no room for Billy and Danny." Weeks later he was persuaded to stay the night. On return to the nursery he rushed in to Billy and Danny and said, "You see, I have come back." On another occasion he said, "When I am grown up I am going to have somewhere to live and I am going to take Billy and Danny and all the other children to live with me."

Billy, aged nine, was a bed-wetter and generally intractable. With matron's consent I brought his sister Mary from a neighbouring Home, distant thirty miles, to stay two nights. The children were shy at first, but very proud of each other. The other children were enormously interested in the meeting and "showed off" the sister to everyone who came. They now write to each other regularly. Billy talks a great deal about Mary. There has been important progress in his behaviour.

Albert, aged twelve, was maintained in a private school for maladjusted children. The psychiatrist recommended that some attempt should be made to link him up with his parents and half-brother, and the local authority took great trouble to trace them. This was resisted by the proprietress of the school. With reluctance she allowed the half-brother to visit. Afterwards she claimed that the experience was too upsetting to Albert. She said that Albert had no interest in his own family and was being integrated into hers. Then a former acquaintance happened to meet Albert in the street. He had not seen her for many months. The first thing he said was, "Do you know they have found my brother?"

There was no doubt that Albert's relations with his half-brother contained from time to time elements upsetting to him, for example when a visit came to an end. The problem here recalls the out-worn controversy, should children in hospital be visited by the parents, although they are so upset by the partings? Human relationships in or out of the family cannot be sterilised to prevent the development of painful elements which are as much a part of the relationship as their happier experiences in it. To come to terms with both sets of experiences is in the nature of maturation, and there is no evidence that problems of visiting like Albert's are beyond the power of a child to assimilate with the helpful co-operation of his guardians.

Experience shows that once families are split up it is difficult to reunite brothers and sisters. The effort is always worth making, but results may be disheartening. Time is better spent making careful plans in advance to prevent their being separated. Often these efforts at reunion take place at a time when one or other member of the group is adolescent or nearly adolescent. At such a time the young person in the ordinary family is beginning to step off into life outside the family and is likely to be more than usually two-minded about family ties. Efforts to re-establish family life for the broken family can founder on this rock.

Joan, aged sixteen, had been brought up in a children's Home in the country and did not know of her sister's existence. The children's officer got in touch with the sister, aged nineteen and married, and the two sisters were introduced. The elder sister shared Joan's resentment against her upbringing. One night Joan stayed out late and said she was afraid to go back to matron. She went instead to her sister, who harboured her for a few days and then sent her off. Joan was discovered some weeks later living as a prostitute. It was unrealistic to expect the elder sister to be a "little mother" to Joan, without considerable help in mastering her own family resentments.

In other cases attempts at reunion founder because it has already cost the child a great effort to learn to do without his brothers and sisters; effort which has largely gone into stifling and denying how much he misses them. Re-cementing has to take place in a very secure background indeed, to encourage the child to believe that it is safe and worth while to begin to care again.

A family of six children were committed for neglect. Three of them were boarded out within a few miles of each other. The eldest girl, who has since moved away and been joined by an older brother, makes considerable efforts to continue in touch with a younger brother and sister. But efforts by child care officers to persuade the two older children to visit two remaining members of the family from whom they have been parted for longer have not succeeded, although the committee have offered to pay their fares.

Careful planning can, however, result in happier reunions:

Pamela, aged sixteen, and *Jean*, aged thirteen, had been evacuated ten years previously. They were parted from each other and lost touch with their family. Only after Pamela had left school and started on her nursing career, and Jean had left her foster home, were the sisters reintroduced. They were both eager to get in touch with their family and they helped each other to trace their grandmother. It was foreseen that Pamela would be much less ready than Jean to become dependent upon the family. The child-care officer was not surprised when Pamela rejected the opportunity to spend a holiday with Jean at the grandmother's. Instead of remonstrating with Pamela, the officer took Jean to the grandmother herself. She shared Jean's happiness at finding her family while at the same time, she understood how differently Pamela must feel.

The separated child's apparent rejection of his parents

Again and again the staff of Homes report that children appear to renounce interest in their parents or to reject angrily any approach which the parents may make. The vehemence of the rejection is a measure of the stress the child has undergone on learning to do without them.

> *Mary*, aged five, had been abandoned by her mother in a private foster home two years previously. She was received into a children's Home and repeatedly said, "I hate my mother." Some months later she was restored to her mother and, on seeing her for the first time again, she rushed forward and threw her arms round her mother's neck.

The skilled staff of a reception Home would recognise the significance of Mary's earlier remarks about her mother and would help her to come to terms with her feelings; they would equally well recognise that the child's exuberance at return might not survive unscathed when she settled again to family life.

What is not so frequently recognised as an unspoken protest against being apparently deserted by parents is the child's show of indifference when they visit. This was vividly portrayed in the film, *A Two-year-old goes to Hospital*. James Robertson describes the two-year-old child's reaction in his book *Young Children in Hospital*.

> "On the third day her mother visits, but although *Laura* has wanted her so much she makes no attempt to get to her. Her natural spontaneity towards her mother has been frozen. She seems to have doubts about her mother's good will towards her. . . . When her mother leaves, Laura turns her head away. She does not understand the medical necessity, and for her this is an experience of rejection by her mother."

Still less is there a general recognition of the way in which a child covers his feeling of being rejected by appearing to be preoccupied with the material gifts which the parents bring on their visits.

> In Court the matron of a Home gave evidence that *Ronald*, aged ten, had showed little interest in his parents when they visited and had "only wanted them for the sweets and presents they brought him".

Yet Ronald had lived all his life with his parents up to the time of his committal six months earlier and was delighted when the Court allowed him to return to them.

James Robertson describes similar behaviour in a child who had been some weeks in hospital.

Barbara, aged two-and-a-half had been in hospital for some weeks. She no longer showed disturbances on her parents' weekly visits. When she saw them arrive her face lit up, not, apparently, for their own sakes but because of the diversion they brought, in much the same way as she might greet me if I had a sweet in my pocket. She dug into her mother's bag and enjoyed the toys and sweets she found there; but she showed no warmer interest in her parents than in the transient nurse.

Children in modern, well-equipped establishments, too different from their own homes, often have problems connected with these standards.

Shirley, aged ten, was brought up in a comfortable and well-furnished children's Home. Then she had a chance to return to her family. After a trial week-end at home, she said to matron, "Why doesn't my mummy have any carpets in her house?" Matron helped her over this difficulty by saying, "You don't have carpets in every house. When I was a little girl, I didn't have carpets either."

Separation can often only be borne by adults if the importance of what has been lost is minimised, and if the value of what is being got in its place is exaggerated. Probably this factor coloured Shirley's attitude.

The child's need for tangible links with his family

The following story speaks for itself:

David was an exceptionally delicate baby and he was placed by the local authority in a private nursery which gave good material care. His mother died in a sanatorium when David was four. She had had no contact with him and David was not told of her death. The time came when David had to leave the nursery and an attempt was made to place him with a specially experienced foster mother who had herself been a nursery matron and had retired on marriage. David almost at once attempted to set fire to the foster home. At ten years old he came to the reception Home where it was found he needed no prompting to ask about his own family. An intensive search was instituted via the sanatorium where the mother had died. His dead mother's adoptive parents were found, and though they themselves were unwilling to be reminded of her or to have anything to do with David they did provide a photograph of his mother, which David was delighted to have and which he showed to everyone who visited the Home.

David was then introduced to a nurse at the sanatorium who had known his mother well and had warm memories of her. David asked to know where his mother was buried, and a visit was paid to the cemetery in company with the matron of the reception Home, in whom David had confidence. The rector who had conducted the funeral met David and the matron and showed them the grave and gave David a copy of his baptismal certificate with his mother named as godmother. David stayed fourteen months in the reception Home while these enquiries were going on. Then he approached the children's officer and said he had been there much longer than any other child and asked to be moved to a Family Home where another boy had gone. He has now been two years in the Family Home. His emotional condition seems to be considerably improved and his school work is better.

The homeless child's search for parents in adolescence

Many children who have lost touch with parents begin to search for them when they are old enough.

June was placed privately in a foster home by her own mother at the age of two. The mother visited for two or three years and then disappeared. Payments were made to the foster mother by the local authority. Eleven years later, at the age of sixteen, June began to ask the child care officer about her mother. She had often previously asked her foster mother and had never been satisfied with the answers. Three years later, at nineteen, her questions were satisfied. Her mother was traced through the Assistance Board to a distant town. The mother was seen by a child care officer and was found to have living with her another illegitimate child, now aged nine. June was told of her mother's existence, but not about the half-sister. June at her own request was taken to visit her mother. The mother herself, by previous arrangement, told June about the half-sister and introduced them. The foster mother had always denigrated June's mother to her and was opposed to any reunion. June is now aged twenty-five, married, with a child of her own. She says that had she known about her half-sister she probably would not have chosen to visit her mother, but there is little doubt in the minds of the workers concerned that June would never have been satisfied until she had found her mother again and that relatively little harm had been done by the discovery of the half-sister.

Albert has been referred to before, as a boy who attached importance to the discovery of his half-brother. Six years later he had left the private school and gone into lodgings. Strenuous efforts by the child care officer to trace his mother (including a visit to his putative father over a hundred miles away) had yielded no result. One Christmas, when he was seventeen, Albert wrote off to the address given on his birth certificate. The letter was forwarded to his maternal grand-mother and by her to his real mother, who replied within a week from another part of the country. She had married and had two children, but she and her husband were willing to have Albert for a visit. After a week-end visit Albert accepted his mother's and step-father's invitation to live with them. He was warned by the child care officer that he would find this mode of life difficult and probably unsatisfactory, but he was determined to give it a trial. Albert returned four months later, having parted with his mother by mutual consent, but without recriminations. The family on their part, although they had found it a strain, had been willing to give the arrangement a more prolonged trial. Mother and son still correspond occasionally and Albert gave his mother's name and address as next-of-kin when he joined the Army. Now he has re-established a relationship with his mother, he is planning to keep in touch with his grandmother and his half-brother as well.

It is clear that to attempt to put mother and child in contact after a long period during which the mother has, deliberately or not, lost contact with the child must involve the most careful thought for the best interests of both parties. This will be particularly necessary if the child is illegitimate and the mother was married at the time of his birth, or if she has subsequently married. Child care officers approach the task of tracing such a mother with special concern for her interests and those of her new family. Whether the circumstances allow of a reunion or not, the removal of doubt about the fate of her child is frequently acknowledged as a relief by the mother.

Peter Stokes was born to a married woman, his father being a coloured soldier. When Mr. Stokes returned from the armed forces he insisted on Peter's being sent away to a children's Home. Fifteen years later Peter asked the child care officer to find his mother, and she was traced to a distant town. The child care officer called at the house, exercising great care to ensure that he spoke to Mrs. Stokes alone and not to reveal his identity and mission to anyone else in the house. Mrs. Stokes was shocked at first, but after a long talk she said she had never forgotten about Peter and had always wondered anxiously how he was faring. She asked for time to think about it, and some weeks later she wrote to say she had told her husband and grown-up children that she was in touch with Peter again. She later visited Peter in his lodgings and gave him a present of a travelling clock, which is now his most prized possession. With Mr. Stokes' approval Peter visits the family for the day about twice a year and his half-brother has invited him to stay for a week's holiday with his wife and family. Mrs. Stokes has repeatedly expressed relief at seeing Peter again and knowing that he is getting on all right.

CHAPTER THREE

THE ESSENTIALS OF FAMILY LIFE

What does the family do for the child?

IF THE FAMILY means so much to the child that he is under excessive strain when he has to do without it, it is pertinent to explore the actual gains from family life, and the rôle played by the parents, which is so difficult for other adults to take over.

When we try to sift the principles underlying satisfactory child development, we find at once that we are dealing with strong emotional needs through which the child makes very primitive demands on the parent. The nature of these demands changes during the first few years of his life, but vestiges of them remain even when maturity is reached. Later growths, of course, achieve greater prominence in the picture.

The very young baby looks to the parent to protect him from the discomforts of pain and hunger and to provide the simple pleasures of food, sleep and warmth. If these things are present, he is content, and if they are absent, he is cross and anxious. At this stage one woman may not be hard to replace by another, but a changing rota of different women adds grave uncertainty and anxiety to the child's life.

In a very short time the child feels assurance that his wants will be satisfied from the very presence of the mother. Mother and child both want the same thing, the child's well-being. Such an identity of interest is hard to find again anywhere in life. The child learns to depend on it. Companionship and trust develop over feeding, bathing, bedtime and the playtimes which go with all these. This link between bodily care and loving care is a basic one in understanding children's needs. If the mother goes away at this stage, the child is thrown into a state of anxiety and for the time no other woman will really do.

A personal ideal

When this link is present, the child soon knows when the father and mother are displeased, and he is unhappy about it. Fear of their displeasure is one of the strongest forces in moving him to lessen his demands and to choose proper times and places to make them, even to give up some of them entirely as being too primitive and displeasing. He learns new ways of behaviour and adopts new pleasures because the parents wish it. So the parent becomes the loving provider of more civilised interests. He has an exaggerated idea of their goodness and power: "My mummy is the best mummy in the world: my daddy is the strongest." He likes to be associated with them in activity; to do the housework with mother and help father with the garden or to clean the shoes, and he adopts many details of their habits and ways. Out of this realisation of the parents' continuous protection and his assurance that they will stand by him, even when he is naughty, grows the wish to be like them in every way. "Being good" means being like the parents not only when they are present, but in his own secret life.

Sustaining the ideal

From sharing tasks with his parents the child learns to share their attitude to work. In so far as they are his ultimate authorities his attitude to them will pattern his attitude to authority in adult life. Family feeling is thus the basis of social discipline, and anything which threatens it in childhood threatens the inner structure on which his attitude to civilised values will depend when he is mature. The child's early attitudes to his father and mother will be the basis of all his ideals, and he will draw strength from his feelings towards his parents to sustain his ideal now, and on into life. Contrariwise, if the parents go away from him at an early age there is always the danger that his standards, built around their constancy, will deteriorate. It takes a long time for a new relationship with another adult to be built up, and not until this attains a strength comparable with the old one will the child be able to resume those standards and those attitudes to civilised ways which the parents' going broke up for him. The interim period may be one of silent misery or one of active revolt. It depends on whether he is more afraid than angry or more angry than afraid. In both cases he is bound to feel that there are two types of people in the world, children and adults, and that their interests are in conflict.

Of course, the child is not a realist, and the height of his ideals is not altogether to be measured by the real social qualities of his parents, but rather by the devotion they can inspire. It is often said that any home, even the worst, may be better than no home at all. This is, of course, very different from saying, "A child should never be removed from his home, however bad that home is." We must examine most carefully the substitute care which we are likely to be able to provide, and not remove a child from his home without the reasonable assurance of being able to provide a substitute which will better serve his needs.

First steps in community life

The most fundamental modification which the child has to make on the basis of his love for his parents is in his desire to have them exclusively to himself and to thrust away all possible rivals. In a growing family, such rivalry presents the parents with one of the most urgent daily problems. It is dealt with in part because in the child's wish to be like the parent there is implicit the desire to love what the parent loves, including the other children. But the average parent knows how many hard battles are fought before the child is willing to accept, not an exclusive, but an equal place in the family. When he does accept it, it is because he has come to realise that it is a condition of the continued love of his parents, and in this way he makes his first step in accepting community life for their sakes.

No real group life is possible to a child who has abandoned the hope of intimacy with a beloved adult person. Living together is an extension of family life, and good relationships with one's equals presuppose a common bond with an affectionate, just, parent. Otherwise, competitive, jealous or envious elements always dominate the child's relationships and he either retires from the group or struggles aggressively to destroy it. The family provides him with as much rivalry as he can well bear. If it is large, there is a possibility of older children who will mother him. One thing is certain about an ordinary family—it cannot contain a large number of children all about the same age, all demanding exactly the same thing from the adult. In the family, he can make the step to community living, admittedly with difficulty, but the task is a possible one.

Access to the larger community

The next steps are usually easy. A home is generally rooted in a neighbourhood and the parents' neighbourly contacts naturally become the child's. In this extension of the family circle the child finds his own special place and opportunities. He goes to relatives and neighbours for consolation and occupation if home proves temporarily neglectful or unsympathetic. (This goes unnoticed in an ordinary family, but tends to arouse outside comment in a substitute home.) The neighbourhood supplies activities which supplement the home and feed his growing desire to venture outside it. He transfers to the homes of his friends and neighbours the standards of behaviour he has learned in his own. He even supplements these standards from outside the family and enlarges his ideal of what he wishes to become. This is so gradual a process that he does not feel suddenly plunged into an alien world, nor is the divergence between family and community standards harshly or suddenly held up to him. Family life is a stepping-stone to community life, and as he grows older the community offers him the more complete satisfaction which the family can no longer do. He can escape spiritually from the home while retaining his deepest roots within it and he has the exultant feeling of achieving a separate new personal quality in his life into the bargain.

A personal life with activities and possessions

This need for a personal quality in interests and experience extends to the activities the child undertakes—for example, to his play and to the things he collects, often valueless in themselves but specific to him. A teacher once commented on a box of personal junk a child had collected: "Rob has parked a lot of himself out in that box." This "parking out" of oneself, the direction of interests and knowledge, is the basis of culture. For example, the connoisseur collects and grows knowledgeable at the same time about pictures and books. Culture is not imposed by lessons or even by a cultivated environment, but by the feelers the child puts out to draw the outside world into himself.

The following report, which came from a Home for boys aged eight to fourteen, shows how a general insight into their needs can modify a detail of procedure to the great benefit of the children.

The boys had weekly carpentering classes in a workroom, but only when each boy was given a few tools of his own and began chipping at odd pieces of wood all over the house and garden, did they really "take up" carpentry. The carpentry efforts took the place of endless day-dreaming and periods of apparent detachment in which the children had earlier given the impression of being "all inside and inaccessible".

Fortunately, this once common state of mind of children in Homes is found less and less. The contrast between the aims and flexibility of the new and the old kinds of régime is pointed if one remembers what passed for occupation in former times.

In the desire to ensure that a large number of children had exercise in the fresh air without using the time of too many staff and without losing control, it was common to take groups of children on aimless walks. If one were looking for a mode of punishing children one could hardly find anything more effective. On the other hand, nowadays a walk to some specific place in a group of two or three with a grown-up is often regarded as a treat.

The family provides the child with a natural way of developing towards civilised community life. Any mode of upbringing which aims to model itself on the family and to produce similar results must seek therefore to provide the child with those features of family life which are essential to his age. These are:

A close and continuous relationship with one woman who will provide bodily care in such a way as to attach to herself the child's love and admiration, and to stimulate him to trust and assurance and a desire to become progressively more like the adult.

A father figure, preferably in the relationship of husband to the woman who provides care; or failing that, a devotion to the idea of a father as exemplified by the presence in his environment of one or more men who can command his affection and his admiration and the respect of the woman looking after him.

A small community life in a reasonably stable group of not more than eight to ten children of mixed ages. Here he can fight successfully his battles with jealousy and envy because the competition is not over-whelming, provided he is helped by something akin to parental understanding.

Opportunity for freedom and diversity in activities, possessions and occupations and in the spending of leisure.

Access to a larger community or neighbourhood in whose life he can participate.

An affectionate, stimulating, controlling and understanding environment in which his urge to become progressively independent will be tolerated and encouraged.

CHAPTER FOUR

THE SUBSTITUTE HOME AND THE CHILD'S OWN FAMILY

How does a Home differ from a family?

To MAKE REALISTIC plans for running children's Homes it is necessary to face the fact that, both in the minds of the staff and in the minds of the children, there are certain differences between a children's Home and a family. For example, the staff expect to retire eventually and to hand the children on to their successors, and the children know this. They know, too, that children come and go and that they cannot expect to remain as a stable, companionable group. This could only be achieved if each child were to remain until he grew up and left to make a home of his own. The children are not related by blood to the staff, and are generally not related to each other.

Have we, therefore, written this book under the impetus of some idealistic fervour? In these circumstances is there any sense in talking about making a home out of a Home? Supposing we can manage to link the concept of home with the concept of a Home and retain the thesis of this book more or less undamaged, we must acknowledge that the staff are not the parents of the children and that the relationships are relatively impermanent.

We can draw a parallel (though by no means a complete one) which may illustrate the situation. A number of people living together in a ship make a series of complicated relationships which are broken at the end of the voyage with some pain, some disappointment and some relief. If the voyage has been a long one these relationships are firm enough to give rise to sincere feeling and many backward looks. This community of people have kept each other warm and stimulated. After they have settled back into their wider life ashore the passengers may realise something of the exaggerated feeling which infused their life on board and they may laughingly readjust their conceptions of its importance in the renewed reality of the homes to which they have returned. Nevertheless, there are few of us who do not look back on a pleasant voyage as a permanent enrichment of experience.

To return to our children. They come to us without their families, in a state of deprivation, very different from the holiday mood of the traveller. The two situations have, however, one thing in common: both sets of people are cut off for the time being from the background and bases of their ordinary lives, and to some extent this makes them more ready to avail themselves of the relationship provided in the new situation. We do not forget that we have emphasised in this book why constant deprivation may make a child unwilling to make new relationships. The human mind can contain simultaneously many opposing forces, and at this point we are concerned only to emphasise that, like the voyager, the child has need of human relationships and that this need can be met in a way which will benefit the child's emotional growth.

It is not necessary for staff and children to enter into a common fantasy that they are going to be together permanently or that the Home is to be equated with the homes they have lost. It is better to emphasise that the child's capacity to make and enjoy relationships continues and can be encouraged: that the child needs someone who will try to give him some of the things which he has a right to ask from parents, and that in their rôles as guiding adults the Home's staff declare their willingness to give.

We have said that growing up in the Home is not continuous and that the children are not all biologically related to each other and to the staff, and therefore cannot feel so secure as in a family. A Home can only be a limited approximation to a family, but it is an approximation to which effort can profitably be directed. Such effort may make all the difference between producing a child who is humanly capable and integrated around human values and a child who is cynical, or less integrated. The outcome will certainly not be identical with an up-bringing in a natural home and, considering the multitude of circum-stances which the children's natural homes cover, we can only say that in some cases it may be better and in some cases it may be worse. Our aim has been to show the kind of upbringing which will be geared not only to structuring the child's outward behaviour and performance, but also to vitalising and replenishing his inner life. (It is our contention that we may achieve the first of these aims without accomplishing the second, and in so doing produce a relatively conforming citizen, but not necessarily a man or woman able to live a life in warm human contact with others and with aims and ambitions for himself which take full account of his many human needs.)

But if we are to do this we have to consider that the resources open to us for children in care are different and more limited than for other children in the community, and even that we may have to act differently with these children from how we do with our own children in our own families.

Residential workers know quite well that their aims must be limited in the way we have just discussed. Two considerations have sometimes been put forward by them to suggest that, because we cannot hope to do the same thing as parents with these children, we must even further limit our efforts to cater for their needs. It has been said, for instance, that it is not possible to treat children in a Home as individuals because the children's sense of fairness, dictated by their jealousies, makes this impossible. Children are quick to detect favouritism, based on the adult's emotional attitude to one child compared with another, but they are able to put themselves in the position of other children, either older or younger, and sympathise with the needs of these other children in their different stages of growing up. We should not be misled by their verbal protests. They do not always mean us to act on these protests, and the child who sees extra care being given to the sick child knows very well that this care will be available to him, too, in case of need. The same is true for the extra care given to a depressed, agitated or anxious child. It is, however, necessary to explain to children why we make these differences, and even to elicit their support. This is particularly true when a child's problems are chronic and prolonged.

The second argument, which is often raised to suggest that it is idealistic to hope to give a children's Home the qualities of a family, is that, on the one hand groupings are too large and, on the other, an infiltration of highly aggressive children not easily amenable to discipline precludes a family atmosphere.

These two issues will be discussed in separate sections of this book. At this point we would agree that they may become overridingly difficult features. We will be at pains, in the separate chapters devoted to these topics, to show how the policy of a child-caring agency can operate to prevent the needs of the majority of more normal children being sacrificed to this small group.

With the foregoing provisos and limitations we should like to consider some ways in which a residential establishment can preserve some of the essentials of a child's family feeling.

The first essential must surely be to manifest to the child the staff's respect for his feelings towards his real parents and the staff's desire to keep in touch with the real parents for their own sakes as well as for the children's.

Contacts with parents

It will already be clear that the child's feelings towards his parents or towards the memory of his parents are of fundamental significance in determining his attitude to life as he grows up.

Careful planning can often keep children within regular visiting reach of their parents, but if this proves impossible the staff of the Home can do something to ensure that they remain in the child's memory. It is enormously important that the contact should be reciprocal and that the feeling should be deepened by letters, parcels and visits and by offering every encouragement to the parent to keep up with the child's developing interest and progress. Where there is an adequate staff of child care officers, time can be spent in escorting children to see parents and to stay for holidays with them.

In small Homes it is possible for matrons to write to the child's parents from time to time, giving an account of his progress and enclosing photographs and school reports. On occasion, when no reply has been received for as long as a year, the absence of the accustomed letter may bring the first reply—a protest at the omission—clearly showing that the letters had at least kept alive the parents' interest, and that they now miss them. It is helpful if administrative arrangements are sufficiently flexible not to interfere with a free contact between the matron and the child's parents. There will generally be other contacts with the parent as well; there may be regular visits to collect parents' financial contributions and also visits of caseworkers to help the parents modify their feelings and their circumstances. These need not interfere with the equally important contact between the parents and the people who have the daily care of their children; for this it is vital that there should be the fullest confidence between the residential and the field workers. Keeping contact is a team effort.

We may well ask, however, how much of this contact percolates to the child and even so how far it satisfies his hunger to know what is happening in his family? The work of the most imaginative agency must be seen to be pitifully inadequate in practice. Only the child's hunger for love and recognition from his family and the painful sensitiveness of his imagination enable him to make something of this poor fare. But there is no substitute for direct contact between parents and children.

Often the emotional condition of the parents is such that the impetus to maintain the contact has to come from the matron rather than from the parents. Where there is a good relationship between parents, matron and child, the parents' visits are welcomed, and every help is given to make them regular and enjoyable.

Alexander, aged four, was admitted to a residential Nursery when his pregnant mother was deserted by her husband. Twins were born to the mother, and she had to stay in welfare accommodation for many months with them because she had nowhere to live. Matron spoke regularly on the telephone to the mother and the child care officer brought her and the twins to visit Alexander as often as possible. At Christmas-time one of the staff turned out of her bedroom and made it available for mother and twins to stay for a night at the Nursery. Alexander was left in no doubt that he would go and live with her one day. After months of negotiation with the housing department and the Assistance Board the family was installed in a council house where they have now been for several years and are doing tolerably well.

Leslie, aged five, and his two younger brothers and sisters were (through shortage of vacancies) placed in a Nursery 200 miles from their parents, when they were evicted for not paying the rent. Matron wrote to the parents regularly, but received no reply until, after several months, a visit was made to them by a child care officer. The father was given the money to visit the children, but on the first occasion he used it instead to go off to a cycle rally. After more months of correspondence the parents were visited again, this time with a railway warrant and an invitation from matron for Leslie's mother and the baby to come and stay for three nights in the Nursery. Lodgings for the father were found in the village. This visit inaugurated a new era in the family relationships. With quickened interest in their children the parents were stimulated to pay off their arrears and apply for a fresh council house. This was eventually made available and matron and one of the staff took the children home and spent several hours settling them in. Matron has visited them once or twice since.

Pam and Amy, aged thirteen and eleven, were placed in a Family Home 180 miles from their parents. This removal was decided upon because the father had been convicted of offences against another daughter on the occasion of a visit he paid to her in a Home. Their mother was unable to write and she had another younger child to look after at home. She and older brothers sent Christmas cards once a year. After several years matron sent an invitation to mother to come and stay for a week, bringing the youngest child with her. The mother proved unable to plan how to spend the days, but matron fixed up everything for her, putting her on the bus to the seaside, sending the family off to the pictures on a wet day and so on. The girls are likely to remain away from their parents for good, but it was felt to have been helpful for them to have seen their mother as a real, living person.

Use can be made of the telephone if the child is taught in advance how to use it.

Diane, aged six, and *Christine*, aged four, came into a Nursery when their mother died. In this Nursery it was the practice for all the older children in turn to speak to "their" child care officer on the telephone from time to time. Consequently, Diane and Christine knew all about telephones after a few days. Arrangements were then made for them to speak almost every night to the grandfather and grandmother, who lived a few miles away. They were subsequently boarded out with relatives.

The Nursery school can play a part in encouraging contact between child and parent. Children can paint pictures and make Christmas cards to be sent to their fathers and mothers. Use can be made of photographs; both the dispatch of photographs of the children to quicken the parents' interest and the provision of photographs of parents for the children to keep.

Even when parents have abandoned or deserted the children or are chronically ill in hospitals for mental disorder, there are many ways of making the parents real to the children. One Hospital Board makes arrangements for mothers who are severely sub-normal to make up a party to go and visit their children in Homes and Nurseries once or twice a year. If special care is taken it is often possible for children to visit their parents in mental hospitals. This calls for close co-operation between the staff of the hospital and the children's department to ensure that a time is chosen when the patient is at her best and to make the visiting arrangements as smooth and sheltered as possible. Some psychiatric social workers arrange to bring individual patients from the hospital to visit their children in the Homes. The children are helped to understand their parents' condition by talking to them in a matter-of-fact way about their parents' being in hospital because they are ill.

Bulletins about the patients' progress can be passed on to the children, especially when they are encouraging. The experience of some children's departments has been that children of mentally ill patients often have a noticeable drive towards being stable and well behaved themselves and that this can be depended upon to enable them to understand the bizarre and disturbing behaviour of a parent if they are given an adequate explanation. It seems that a child can accept this direct and realistic approach to the facts of mental illness because it is more reassuring than the anxious imaginings with which they otherwise endow the condition.

In the rare case of the genuine foundling child whose parent is never traced, the clothing and any articles which the mother leaves with the child can be preserved. In after years he can at least say, "This is something which my mother handled and gave to me."

Problems in the relationship between the agency and the family

Formal visiting days are not always conducive to good family relationships. The best Homes and Nurseries encourage parents to come when they can and put themselves to considerable trouble to make visits successful. One of the unsatisfactory features of mass visiting days is the effect they have on those children who never receive a visitor. Of course, it is helpful to try to get parents to give notice of intended visits so as not to upset the running of the Home and to ensure that the child is available to be visited.

> *John*, aged twelve months, lost several fingers through parental neglect and was committed to care by the Court. His mother travels 120 miles on Sundays at least once a month to visit him. She has to make several changes of public transport and to take with her the other four children who are all under ten years old. Matron has repeatedly urged Mrs. D. to try to come on Saturday and to leave some of the other children at home. Nevertheless, she is always heartily welcomed when she turns up on Sundays. In between visits Mrs. D. telephones matron twice a week, always late at night when her husband has got home from the public house and she is free to go to the phone-box.

Nowadays, heads of Homes are given opportunities when possible of seeing the homes from which their children come. They pay visits with child care officers and sometimes accompany children when they are restored to their parents. They are able to appreciate the parents' difficulties and the conditions under which they are obliged to bring up their families. They are getting an understanding of the kind of mental disability which handicaps parents in providing proper upbringing.

All of us are inclined to be resentful of the actions of parents, which have resulted in their children's coming into public care. We can acknowledge that there is always a proportion of families which get into this kind of situation. If we are able to concentrate upon the strengths rather than the weaknesses of such parents we are more likely to help them to the point at which they can become effective parents again. We do a disservice to the children if we drive parents into still greater ineptitude by underlining their weaknesses, or if we keep them from visiting their children, by words or gestures of condemnation. Many a parent has walked up and down outside a children's Home on visiting day and has failed to summon courage to go in.

Handling the child's feelings about his family

We have to be watchful to avoid conveying to a child any disapprobation of his parent. This is especially necessary when a court has committed a child because of some defect in upbringing by the parent. Examples are the committal of children who have been victims of offences of indecency within their own family circle, and of those who have been brought by their own parents before the court as beyond control.

In our anxiety to undo the corruption which we may feel the child has suffered in the process of his upbringing, it is easy to do more harm than good. Such a child is beset with intense conflict. From the very fact of his removal from home he is left in little doubt about society's judgment on his parents and, in most cases, he will also feel that this is society's judgment on him too. The immediate problem of the Home is to accept him and to try to create conditions which will integrate him into the new community. If the individual child is accessible to influence it will be on the basis of the relationship which has been made with him. It may only be long after his admission to the Home that the child will be ready to talk about these family disturbances to a person in whom he has learned to repose confidence. At this point one becomes aware of the intense anxieties which events, and his own part in them, have set up in him and which only then he is willing to share. Premature criticism of himself and his family will only strengthen his fight for self-esteem in unsatisfactory ways. He may withdraw into isolation or into a defiant "don't care" attitude. If for any reason these matters have to be taken up with him prematurely he can be brought to understand that the decision has rested with the court and that his admission to the Home and his care within the Home must comply with the court's directions.

It is for this reason that many children's departments are reluctant to receive voluntarily into care children whose circumstances are such that they should be brought before a court on the grounds that they are neglected or beyond control. The children who are properly received under a voluntary arrangement are those whose parents are dead or ill or who have disappeared or who are palpably prevented from looking after the children. Whenever the grounds for admission to care are different, and the parent appears to the child to be in a position to have him at home, it is difficult for the child to understand why he has to stay away from his family. If the reasons are rooted in the personality and behaviour of the parents or of the child and not in external circumstances, Parliament has provided for action to be taken through the court. The child, as he grows up, may or may not feel that the decision of the court was a fair one, but at least he will be able to understand that neither his parents nor those looking after him are capriciously keeping him away from home.

Children's Departments are sometimes pressed to receive children voluntarily into care in circumstances where court action would be more appropriate. It is no kindness to the child to disregard the law and to attempt to make instead an insecure voluntary arrangement which will be puzzling to the child and which may break down at a moment of crisis.

Staff of Homes will often welcome the help of specialists when children want to discuss their parents' behaviour. Some older children get preoccupied with their parents' part in bringing about their present situation and with their parents' attitudes towards them. They need time and skilled help to work out their feelings and to direct them into channels which will assist their emotional growth. The special skill of the staff of Homes is that they are able to go on looking after the child day by day without getting too involved in those complex matters which can best be dealt with by child guidance clinics and by child care officers.

Doris, aged nine, was received into care at the request of her father. Her mother had deserted years before and Doris and her father had lived together in a variety of unsuitable lodgings. He felt he could no longer manage her, and Doris went to a Reception Home, where he was encouraged to visit. A month later Doris alleged that her father had interfered with her when he took her out. He was sentenced to six months' imprisonment for indecent assault. Doris was committed to the care of the County Council and was transferred to a family Home after an unsuccessful introduction to a potential foster parent. The father's offence against Doris caused strong feelings in those who had the daily care of the child; they felt he had done her irreparable harm and they pointed to her undoubted sexual precocity as a consequence. They felt he had forfeited his parental rights by such an action and that only harm could come by allowing the contact to continue. In contrast to this, the child care officer, Miss S., was convinced that Doris' only relationship of any intensity was with her father. She had no other interested relatives, and her father was devoted to her, though he was immature in his affections and criminally perverse in his indulgence. Miss S. believed that Doris would suffer greatly if the link were broken entirely. After lengthy discussions, a compromise was finally agreed upon. Miss S. was to control Mr. A.'s visiting of Doris. He was to come once a month on a Saturday afternoon in the company of Miss S., and together they were to take Doris out. This plan was closely adhered to. It was not plain sailing, however; the residential staff noted that Doris played upon her father's sympathy, complained about the Home and so on. Sometimes her behaviour deteriorated when her father had visited. She reverted to enuresis and to sulking. The father had moods of rebellion, when he became angry against the staff of the Home and wrote foolish letters to Doris. But through all this, visiting continued.

The success of the plan depended on a number of factors. The child-care officer was fortunate in having sufficient time to give to the problem, not only in having available one Saturday afternoon in four, but also in having time to give to assist the father in a painful process of rehabilitation when he came out of prison. He had been brought up in a vast orphanage. He had not seen his parents since he was six. He was immature and extremely dependent—would ring up Miss S. to tell her he had changed into winter woollies! At other times he wrote angrily "I thought you were a friend, but now I know you're not." At first he relied on her assistance in finding jobs and lodgings, but gradually became much more independent, deciding to move to a distant mining job, but still writing regularly and visiting monthly. His dependence made it possible to ensure his co-operation in visiting regularly and keeping to the plan. Had he been a violent man, or so hostile to authority that he refused to comply with the arrangements, the whole story would have been different.

It is perhaps more difficult in smaller things, such as matters of taste in dress, for the staff of the Home not to appear critical of the child's own parents.

Irene, aged thirteen, was presented by her mother with a satin party frock of petunia pink with fawn sleeves. The mother offered this diffidently asking, "Will matron allow her to wear it?" The child care officer said she was sure that matron would make opportunities for the child to wear it, which she does.

Molly, aged eleven, went on for months wearing a worn-out cardigan which was too small for her. Matron was sensitive about this as it might have reflected on the way she dressed the children. However, she understood that Molly wore this garment because it had been given to her by a dearly-loved former foster mother.

In the days of Public Assistance Committees, progressive Superintendents of groups of children's Homes campaigned against the system of using parental visits to check their changes of address for the information of the Treasurer's department to enforce the payment of contributions. This shows how practical understanding of the child's needs can guide the persons who control the administrative machine.

In these days the situation is not likely to arise in this form. Child care officers have many ways of keeping in regular touch with the parents, and it will be rare for a parent's address to be unknown if he is sufficiently in touch with the child to be visiting the Home. If, exceptionally, a parent whose whereabouts were unknown should arrive to visit his child, there will be much that the staff will want to discuss with him. The child care officer will deal with parental contributions as just one of many ways in which the parent is significant in the total situation.

It is often the function of the agency to face both parents and children with the problems of a harsh reality, which they are perhaps unwilling and unprepared to meet. Good team work between residential and field workers can often mitigate the difficulties of this kind of situation, to the extent to which their outlook is insightful and instructed.

CHAPTER FIVE

MAKING A FAMILY ATMOSPHERE IN THE HOME

THE DAILY MANAGEMENT of a children's Home naturally occupies a great deal of the time and thought and effort of the staff. If the staff are aware that the provision of physical care associated with mealtimes, bathtimes, bedtime and dressing provides an opportunity for encouraging both intimacy and independence, they will go a long way towards making a real home. If the housekeeping and house management are undertaken as ends in themselves, many opportunities to bring about homelike experiences for the children will be lost.

Mealtimes

Where grown-ups and children take their meals together and conversation is free and friendly, there is the best basis for family feeling. Wardens not only learn a great deal about the children and their activities during the meal, but themselves set a standard for natural good behaviour and social interchange, which the children willingly adopt. Where this is absent, a feeling of jealous isolation from the adult is often very marked and the standard of the children's behaviour bears the unnatural stamp of being dependent solely on the warden's presence. Behaviour changes immediately he withdraws or ceases to make himself felt. Even when he is present, he may only maintain order by constant nagging.

The following example is from a good Home:

Home for thirty boys, aged seven to fourteen. Mr. and Mrs. X sit down with the boys, and the house matron also has her meals with the group. There is considerable chat between children and staff and the children speak a good deal about their school experiences of the day. There is much laughter. Children take it in turn to remove dishes from tables and fetch cold courses from the kitchen. Hot tureens are brought in by the staff to a side table. Towards the end of the meal any children who have finished are allowed to go at a signal from the warden. The rest stay on till they finish, and slip off individually in turn.

Sometimes the children are isolated at mealtimes from a mistaken sense of fairness and kindness to them.

Boys five to eleven years. When this hostel was first visited, shortly after it had opened, it was found that the staff, in spite of being markedly kind in their attitude to the children, were not having their meals with them. The reason given was that, knowing a good many of the boys had come from residential schools where they had been rather regimented, the staff thought it better if they had their meals alone as they would not feel so watched over.

In the case of young children, there is an even greater sense of loss when they lack the friendly reassurance of the adult sharing their meal-times. The busy women who serve from a side table and watch them assiduously have something of the same effect that a group of waiters in a big hotel may have on an unaccustomed diner. Moreover, the long inactive periods when they sit quietly without occupation and with folded hands beneath the table, place a most unnatural strain on all of them. They make mealtimes burdensome, unpleasant affairs, the strain of which some of them try to escape by eating less and less or refusing food altogether.

In a very progressive and enlightened Nursery the staff did not at first take their meals with the children. This was altered after a child had commented with surprise on seeing a nurse who was off duty eating an apple in the garden. Another child, going into a foster home, had said, "I didn't know grown-ups ate."

The beginning of a meal is a good index to the insight possessed by the staff. Young children in a family do not sit for very long before they are allowed to satisfy their impatience to begin, and mother often starts the toddler on his meal while the older members of the family are getting ready. Certainly he is not kept sitting at the table in anxious expectation before the food is even in the room. It is quite possible to arrange things otherwise.

In most Homes nowadays care is taken to see that the saying of grace does not degenerate into a disciplinary measure to enforce silence at the beginning of a meal nor into a kind of starting signal for an unseemly attack on the victuals. Some Nurseries have a brief grace sung by the children, and in Homes for older children the form of grace may be varied from day to day and it may be said aloud by a different member of the family from meal to meal; or each person may say his own grace quietly to himself. Many clergy do not say a formal audible grace before meals in their own homes and some committees are watchful to ensure that the practice does not become a mere eccentric feature of life in a children's Home long after it has been modified in the homes of the committee members themselves. At least one children's committee, who meet and subsequently have a meal in each of their Homes in turn, have resolved in this respect to defer to the practice of the Home in which they are meeting at the time. It is the example of the adults which counts and the last thing we should want to inculcate would be the idea that there is one code of behaviour for children and another for grown-ups in this respect. We do not want, if we can help it, to per-petuate the attitude of *Molly*, who dutifully said her prayers on the night before she was returning home to her mother for good, and then stood up and announced, with no trace of bitterness, "That's the last time I shall say my prayers: we don't say prayers at home."

Scarcely anywhere in life do individual variations show themselves more plainly than at mealtimes. Zest in meals and good physical growth are clearly related and some wardens are quick to realise this. The following two contrasting examples have been observed in Nurseries:

Each child was given a helping in relation to his appetite and there was no forcing. Almost all the children from eighteen months to two years could feed themselves and, although there was of course a good deal of mess, this was dealt with cheerfully and with under-standing. Some dislikes were tolerated: some children had no gravy, others had their green vegetables as a separate course.

In contrast:

Sister felt strongly that children should be trained to be obedient and to have self-control (e.g. at meals, when the practice has been for every child of the two to five group to be served and then to say, "Thank you, Nurse" before beginning to eat). A child of two, hav-ing had his plate of dinner put in front of him, then had it taken away and placed at the other side of the room because he had not got his hands under the table. He was beside himself with eagerness to start his meal.

Ten years ago it was common to meet harassed and anxious matrons who were extremely disturbed at their inability to coax or force children to eat, and at the worrying loss of weight which the weekly charts presented. Some tried forcible feeding, but confessed that it was unsuccessful. Some who persevered because they did not want to be beaten by the children faced a dilemma when the children started to react to mealtimes by nervous vomiting. We could easily get back to this kind of situation if we allowed our standards of quality and quantity in staffing to drop.

Similar difficulties were caused by other forms of enforced inactivity at meals. One of the pleasures of mealtimes for young children is in being allowed to fend for themselves. Children may be allowed to tie on each other's bibs, help set the table, and help themselves to portions from large dishes. This, however, takes time and much patience. It is always easier and quicker to do everything for the children. Normally active children, denied these opportunities, display their disapproval of enforced inactivity by lassitude, constant crying fits, giving up normal play, and showing restless, preoccupied or supine behaviour. These children often prove incapable of taking their places in family life when they leave the Nursery.

Self-help at mealtimes has sometimes been tried and discarded from the best of motives. It has been found that to serve everybody takes much longer and that the meals dished out first are cold before they are eaten. How many good housewives in ordinary families would not respond to this situation by saying, "Don't wait, anybody."

At one time some matrons put no beakers and water jugs on the table at dinnertime. This was partly because it meant extra work, especially swabbing up spilt water and laundering table-cloths more often, but also because it was found that the children tended to swill their food down without chewing it properly. This tendency would have been dealt with individually instead of by withholding drinking water if there had been sufficient members of the staff for each to have her meals with a small group. When the question was raised the usual reply was that the children could always ask for a drink if they wanted it, but a child in a large poorly staffed group has to limit his demands on the adults to those which he feels are most urgent.

It was probably the belief that enuresis could be reduced by withholding fluids which accounted for the following report:

There is no free access to drinking water, and water is doled out in very limited quantities at stated times. As the heat was intense, children craved water all day and in bed at night, but the routine was not altered. Leslie, whose bodily heat seemed excessive, wailed

in his cot, "No one will give me a drink of water", over and over
again.

By way of contrast, here is a description of another Nursery made at
about the same time:

> Five or six children and one staff sat at each table. Food was served
> in large basins for each table and all the children (aged three to five)
> helped themselves to the amount that each felt he wanted. There
> was lively chatter. The children who were slow eaters were not
> nagged at, but when one or two were left at each table at the end
> of the meal, they were grouped together at one table to finish up
> together.

In an attempt to make meals more homely some Homes have been
provided with separate tables for four or six children. The warden and
staff may distribute themselves amongst the tables or have two or three
children (often the more disturbed ones) to sit at the staff table. In a
small Nursery the family groups may take the main meal at separate
family tables in the dining-room. But tables-for-four are not a *sine
qua non* of good group care and some houseparents, after trying the
experiment, have decided to put the separate tables into a line or a
T-formation so that the whole family of ten or twelve, including the
grown-ups, can sit down together.

It must be recognised that meals with the children make emotional
demands on the staff and, especially in larger Homes, provision is often
made for staff to have some meals in turn, apart from the children.
Similarly, in small Homes where the housefather returns from his
outside work, or where a member of the staff returns from her day off,
it might be an accepted feature that the evening meal is taken separately.
The staff's cooked supper, taken together after the children are in bed,
is a most profitable time for the sorting out of ideas and the knitting
together of staff.

In groups larger than an ordinary family it is generally impossible to
accord the same degree of freedom to talk at mealtimes that would be
allowed in a normal home. This difficulty is not peculiar to children:
any large group of people in one room talking freely tend to raise the
pitch of their voices to meet competition; as witness cocktail parties
and mealtimes at the annual conferences of child care officers. When
good-mannered adults regularly feed together in large groups they
form a habit of speaking more quietly than they do at home. With

children, it is unlikely that such habits will be formed spontaneously, and measures may be taken to impose a régime of quietness. One must sympathise with the writer of the following letter who said in reply to a formal enquiry by the Public Assistance Officer about silence at meals:

"During the twenty years I have been in charge of children's Homes it has never been the practice to command complete silence during meals; at the same time to allow complete liberty of converse would handicap the officers in their duties of teaching table manners; . . . to allow forty children to talk as they wished during meals would seem to me unruly and point to lack of control, without which the child would lose respect for all concerned."

A visitor to the Home commented:

In this Home there is complete silence, which I have "heard". The officers sit apart at meals. The matron and superintendent of this Home once ran a Home for twenty children, where the children called them "Mum" and "Dad". They do not feel they can do that with a larger Home; moreover, they feel that the Committee expects a high standard of behaviour. I think the Committee imperfectly understands the job of the "officers". One member of the Committee, who thought I had criticised the Home, listened for an hour and a quarter while I talked to her about deprived children. She had never thought that it made much difference to children to be moved from their parents, and felt that the job of the Home was to "train" them.

There is some evidence from the school-meals service that difficulties about increasing noise at mealtimes are associated with keeping children waiting at table before and after the service of food. Where the food is served promptly and each child is allowed to leave reasonably soon after he has finished, there is less worry about noise. Apart from the absence of tension when children are not kept waiting, common sense would suggest that they will talk less whilst they have food in front of them.

The secret of happy mealtimes is personal attention. What husband does not miss this when his wife goes out for the evening, even if she leaves a cold supper and everything laid on the table? What housewife does not enjoy the attentions of a restaurant waiter rather than a meal in a cafeteria? Children should, of course, make their contribution to helping at table as well as being the recipients of service, but we can be aware that this is one more sphere is which the child in a large group misses the constant parental attention which is so commonplace as to pass unnoticed in an ordinary household.

Older children can gain a lot from helping to prepare the food sometimes. Their personalities grow in stature if they are allowed to take part in adult activities and to influence the choice of menu. Children can be offered the chance to choose on special occasions, such as birthdays and when a friend or parent is visiting the Home. The children will then feel that food is a topic which can be discussed and that the staff is interested in knowing what they like most.

Food fads are minimised where the feeding arrangements are homely and well ordered. While it is recognised that faddiness is based on a multitude of peculiarities (for example, there are some children whose experiences have caused them to respond with nausea to food which is wet and slippery), yet when the atmosphere at mealtimes is good, and fads are not dealt with by nagging, troubles are reduced to a minimum. In an ordinary family there is a tendency for each member to like what the others like. This sharing of delight in particular things is one of the joyful features of family life.

The giving of sweet things seems to have for many children a special significance which need not necessarily be associated with an exceptional need for sugar in the diet. Staff who recognise this need are careful not to withhold sweet things, either casually or deliberately. In the past, matrons have sometimes maintained a régime of 'no sugar in the tea' on the grounds firstly of rationing and, more recently, because it may be wasted in the bottom of the cup and is therefore best included in foods such as cakes and puddings. This deprivation is the more pointed if some of the staff take sugar in tea or if it is brought out for visitors. Many Homes arrange a small issue of sweets at frequent intervals, in addition to providing pocket money which the children can spend on more sweets if they like. The staff prefer to withhold other treats or privileges, rather than sweets, if it becomes necessary to impose a punishment.

The social value of eating together should not need labouring. The earliest and most significant contact of all human beings is with the mother who feeds them and few important occasions in our grown-up lives pass without the honour of a special meal. The modern adolescent perpetuates this custom in frequenting coffee bars. Eating together offers a lot more than nourishment for the body.

Bathtime and Bedtime

Bath and bedtimes give special opportunities for staff and children to get to know each other. This description of a Nursery in 1946 could be repeated in dozens of Nurseries up and down the country now.

Every member of the staff is on duty for bathing time, and each nurse baths her own group of children. The cook has two children particularly devoted to her and will come on duty to bath these. Bathing is leisurely and every child gets at least twenty minutes' attention so that he can soap and wash himself in part and learn to dispose of his clothing. There is time for fun over bathing. No child is easily willing to be bathed by any other members of the staff than his own. During the rush of the day children can be told, "Save it up till bathtime", when they make an inopportune demand. The children have books in bed after bathing and the staff tell stories and talk to the children about their books. Each child is finally tucked up by his own nurse. They fall asleep fairly quickly.

Bedtime is specially significant for Nursery children, but not only for them. This story is about a Home for older children of the same period.

The rooms each contain four to five children of mixed ages. Some of the little ones sleep in rooms with older boys and the warden says that it makes them particularly protective of these children, so that he finds them "standing up" for their special room-mates in any row during the day and taking the young one's part in any difficulty. I went into one of the rooms before lights out and found in one a boy reading aloud to the rest. In another room a never-ending original story was going on in which each boy took a turn to add a piece of the story. In another room each child was sitting up in bed reading his own book or doing something constructive, such as taking a broken watch to pieces or trying to mend a toy.

If the staff are overworked there is a risk that they will regard bedtime as a period when they are mercifully freed from the children. If children are put to bed too early their only resources in the long, inactive periods before sleep are masturbation, continuous daydreaming, passive resignation or pitting their wits against the staff in clandestine mischief. This has far-reaching effects on the children's reactions at other times and on their general development and character. The following reports describe particular Homes.

In a wartime Home for seventeen boys, aged eight to thirteen. All the boys are in bed by 6.0 p.m. Matron says she herself needs to get to bed early. She has had no holiday in three years and refuses to take one. She complains of the children's sleeplessness and of masturbation. She does not seem to connect excessive masturbation with the boredom of early bedtime and the lack of occupation after this hour.

By contrast:

In a Home for fifteen boys and girls, aged five to fourteen. Matron has been struck by the children's curiosity about her earlier life and present interests and by the dearth of opportunity in a busy day for sharing much of her own life with the children. So she takes it in turn to go each night, after bedtime, to the bedrooms. The children often question her. "What was your mother like?" "Tell us about the time you did so-and-so when you were a little girl." "Why does the Queen travel in a special train?" "Why don't babies have teeth when they are born?" "Do you like the vicar?"

This is what happens in an ordinary family, and the child in a Home wants it too: it is especially the time when adults can help the children in their feelings towards their own parents. Some staff are tempted to put off discussion about the children's own parents, saying that it may upset them and interfere with their sleeping. But children *will* think about their parents; even those they have never seen or heard from, and it is far less disturbing to share with grown-ups the truth about parents than to hug these thoughts to themselves. Children know, of course, when the staff are fearful of, or antagonistic to, their own parents and this exacerbates their already conflicting feelings. A measured presentation of the truth is less disturbing than silence.

Carol, aged four, went with her baby sister to a Nursery when her mother went to a Sanatorium. Six weeks later her mother died. The child care officer, who had taken the children from home to the Nursery in the first instance, asked the staff to tell Carol about her mother's death. A few days later she herself went to the Nursery at bedtime. The nurses said Carol had been told and "hadn't seemed to take much notice". The child-care officer went up and sat by Carol's bed and eventually brought the conversation round to discuss her mother's being in heaven and that Carol would not be seeing her again: that was why Carol and her sister had come to live with Matron. Some weeks later the child care officer was there at bedtime again. Carol said, "I like you. You're the one that tells me about my Mummy."

The child care officer who brings children into residential care has a vital part to play in the adjustment of the child towards his parents. She may be the only person who has been observed by the child to have the confidence of the parents and the only person in his new surroundings whom the child knows to have knowledge of his home and family. She will find that frequent visits to the Nursery at bedtime are most profitable. When parents visit, the staff will be able to take over some part of the child care officer's rôle by letting the child see the good relations that exist between staff and parents and by having a special bedtime talk on the evenings after such visits.

Children may suffer quite needlessly because the grown-ups have no time to talk at bedtime.

Sylvia, aged seven, was received into care with a younger brother and sister whilst mother went to a mental hospital. This was at a time when families were split into Nursery and school-age Homes and Sylvia did not see her brother and sister for some time, nor did she hear from her mother, who was too ill to write. Months later a social worker collected up the three children to take them home to their mother. When Sylvia met her brother and sister in the train she was heard to say, "I often wondered in bed if Mummy was dead."

Of course, there are many evenings in ordinary households when mother is too busy to spare more than a minute or two to each child, especially when there are several children. On the other hand, in a family the child experiences a special kind of privacy in his bath and his bed which is rarely possible even in the smallest groups.

Any child of school age should be at liberty to be in the bath alone if he wants to, subject of course to his being helped to wash adequately and being required to get out within a reasonable time. By ten or eleven he will generally want this, and a little later he is likely to insist on privacy and will expect to have the co-operation of the adults in enforcing this. This kind of sensitiveness, in boys as well as in girls, is being increasingly recognised by the staffs of Homes who find that a tough disregard for the child's feelings has a tendency to make the child even more tough and inconsiderate for others. It is easy to laugh at the adolescents' desire for privacy, and no doubt many boys will later identify with the customs of a group to whom they owe loyalty: in the football pavilion or in the Services. By then an enforced lack of privacy may be more acceptable than it is at the onset of puberty or when a boy has been newly admitted to a Home from the intimacy of his own family. Superintendents of boys' Homes will be specially concerned to protect the new boy from such disturbing experiences.

The need for privacy, however, should not blind us to the fact that even the older children are softer and more amenable at night-time and welcome the nightly visits and confidential talk.

Clothing and appearance

Children value clothing as part of themselves and dislike any system which irons out its individuality, either the possession of clothing in common or the possession of clothing which distinguishes them as institution children, whether it is better or worse than other children's. They specially value the clothing which is given to them as a sign of adult interest and affection and often console themselves by the pretence that a garment is the gift of a parent or nurse.

This is how one Nursery evolved a new attitude to clothing:

At first there was a grave shortage of clothing and the children wore what could be got for them communally. The clothing became badly destroyed and even then they would try to pretend that it was nicer than it was. A girl of four showed me her torn pinafore, and holding together its large rent with one hand and pulling out the dress with the other, she said, "See my pretty frock!" Gradually the children showed preferences for certain articles and were annoyed when other children wore them, and fights over clothing were frequent; or children refused to wear garments which they had seen recently on other children. Finally, under the scheme of group mothers, each child's clothing was bought by the mother, if possible with the help of the child. The group mother often knitted a garment for a child, who took particular interest in it all through its making, frequently showing great pride in its being ultimately for him.

Now clothing cupboards have separate partitions for each child, and children have been found going quietly to look at their store, sometimes selecting in advance what they will wear next. Children frequently take visitors to see their clothing and comment on who gave them this or that garment. Destruction of clothing is now much less common.

In the early stages, children showed their resentment at being communally clothed and their feeling that their clothes belonged to the adult and not to themselves, by deliberately losing garments e.g. shoes would be taken and hidden away. The children would threaten, "I shall lose my shoes." Now the children show themselves upset when garments are mislaid.

In contrast:

A Home for small boys and older girls, about forty in all, was doing excellent work in caring for the children and restoring their self-confidence. For some time in the earlier days, until it was pointed out to them, they were accustomed to sending the children out either to foster homes or to their homes in the ragged and often disreputable clothes in which they had been admitted to the Home. I had the opportunity to observe how each child took this as a sign of being discarded and being no longer of value to the people who had been looking after him.

On the whole the tendency is to spend a good deal of care and money on the standard of Homes children's clothing rather than to skimp. The best of matrons are bound to be affected by public opinion and by the understandable tendency of responsible outsiders to appraise the care which is given to children who are being looked after by strangers.

Home for boys, aged seven to twelve. The children are known in the school as Home children by their very good clothing. They wear boots of excellent quality all the year round and standard grey suits which make them stand out amongst the other children.

Short-stay Home for forty boys and girls over two. I felt rather embarrassed when taking these children home to their parents from the bus stop. As we walked down Commercial Street everyone turned to look at us. The children's clothing was so obviously out of place.

Mixed Home for forty long-stay children. The socks are all marked with the children's names. They are collected every evening after tea and examined and darned when necessary. The child has no responsibility for reporting the need for repair, neither does he ever have the discomfort of a hole in his stocking toe nor get teased for a hole in the heel.

Home for eight school boys. The children are known in the town as

"Mrs. Brown's prep school". They are always dressed in uniform grey jerseys, shorts and turn-over socks. Matron insists on having two of everything in perfect condition so that one child never looks different from all the others.

Home for twenty-five children, mixed ages. The children seem to miss the fun that most people have over new clothes; being admired or respected; discussing whether this or that suits them.

We can give the children smart little turnouts to make them look like other children, but all the clothing in the world cannot make them feel that they are loved. The basis of self-respect and of adherence to acceptable standards of behaviour is a kind of self-love in the true sense of that word. One can only love oneself (as well as others) if one has in turn been loved. The child who is institutionalised from birth may have little self-protectiveness; or self-love in the preservative sense. It is all the more important to see that the provision of clothing is made in an individual, loving way.

Home for twelve children of school age. The children have rough play clothes in which they scuff round the streets, the river bank and the market place on Saturdays. At such times you would never pick them out from the other children in this poor part of the town. They may even have a button missing and holes in their socks, if they have not troubled to ask for these things to be put right. Matron gives a lot of thought and time to the children's clothing: she knits them individual pullovers to patterns they have helped to choose. Care is taken of best clothes and also about the process of handing-down, so that the children understand the value of clothes and that it is a normal economy to transfer clothes which have been grown out of. But the younger children always have some new clothes as well, and are fittingly turned out for each kind of occasion. Matron looks forward to a reduction of numbers in her Home because she wants to give more attention to each child's needs. Incidentally this Home has the lowest clothing costs for the whole county.

The child in a Home is in a peculiar position in so far as he has what the Americans call an alibi for all the unpleasant issues that every child has to face. For example, when the deprived child experiences jealousy and envy because another child has been given something new and he has had to accept something that has been handed down, there is a risk of his saying to himself, "This is done to me because I have no parents to provide for me properly." One of the functions of the staff of a Home is to help in orienting a child to the fact that, although he is in an exceptional situation, he is not necessarily undergoing an exceptional experience. Matron can say, "I know how you feel: that happened to me as a child too because my mother couldn't always let me have the clothes I wanted. I remember . . ." Most matrons nowadays manage not to make the thing unreal by adding, "You are much luckier than I was."

It is fatally easy to criticise the matrons of Homes.

Shirley, aged fourteen, wanted sandals for a school play the following day. Matron was harassed and unsure of herself following a series of upsets which she had had with Shirley. In a moment of exasperation she said, "There is no money in the petty cash to buy you a pair tomorrow." Next day matron found Shirley's house shoes had had the uppers inexpertly cut with scissors. They were now useless for wear as sandals or anything else.

It is too simple to present this story as that of Cinderella, who does her best to fashion the fancy shoes which her harsh stepmother has denied her. A shortage of money for immediate needs comes as no surprise in many ordinary families and many a girl of fourteen expects to borrow or improvise, especially to meet exceptional temporary needs. Shirley could not do this because she was more hurt about being a child in a Home than she was about not having sandals for the school play.

If we can love the children enough to share the normal tribulations of family life with them, the best that can happen is that they will learn to love themselves enough to create in adult life the surroundings for reasonably comfortable and orderly living. Social work with adults often demonstrates how the absence of love in infancy is associated with serious inadequacies in their care of their homes and children.

Mr. and Mrs. C. and their five children were the despair of all the social agencies. Mrs. C. would not take the baby to the clinic; the housing authorities had several times cleared away the rubbish from the wash-house and re-distempered the living-room and kitchen; the neighbours' tolerance had been exhausted; the N.S.P.C.C. were reluctantly considering the removal of the children on grounds of physical neglect. As a last resort a child care officer arranged to call twice a week. At first she took a flit-spray to keep down the midsummer flies, and she suggested that Mrs. C. should attend to a particular cleaning job before her next visit. She made a special appointment at the infant welfare clinic and went with Mrs. C. so that she would not have to sit alone while the other mothers looked disparagingly at her baby. After a few weeks the child care officer stopped talking about such immediate issues. She was offered a specially washed cup at teatime, and the talk was on more general topics. It was several months before Mrs. C. was able to talk about her own childhood. She had been brought up by a grandmother and never understood why her real mother, who lived nearby, seemed to take no interest in her. Mr. C. had lost his mother as a baby and had been brought up by a stepmother. After several years Mr. and Mrs. C. are still living in the same house, and none of their children has had to be removed. Both parents have affection for their children and would resist any attempt to remove them. Mrs. C. still writes at intervals to the child care officer.

Whilst the child care officer could not expect to make profound alterations in character in such adults, it is likely that her intervention enabled the mother to put herself across in the community and to the agencies in such a way as to prevent the break-up of the family. In this instance the mother's lack of self-regard, originating in her childish feeling of being uncared for, might well have led to her children's removal, and thus to a repetition of the pattern for them.

Children in Homes who develop a similarly reproachful attitude to life are no different from other people who have a feeling that they have been denied their birthright. They need help to adjust their own estimate of themselves and to take account of their deprivations and cope with them.

The central principle guiding the provision of clothing for children in Homes is not one of standards, quality or even fitness for fitness sake; it is to use clothing as a mark of individual interest and concern for the child's happiness and well-being. One of the difficulties in the past has been that committees and matrons may have tended to regard the well-turned-out appearance of the children as a test of the care and interest shown by the authorities instead of as an index of the child's self-love. Clothing may tend to represent an extension of the matron's personality instead of expressing the personality of each individual child.

In this respect the care and interest of an expert needlewoman may militate against, rather than in favour of, a feeling on the child's part that he is being clothed lovingly as a mother clothes her own children.

As one public assistance committee superintendent put it, in a published report:

> All girls' clothing is made on the premises and personal choice of colour and style within reasonable limits is encouraged. In effect, each girl has her own personal dressmaker.

In such a set-up there is a risk of all the interest being centred on the achievement of the dressmaker, instead of on the enjoyment that the child should get from her clothes. A dress amateurly run up by a housemother (to a pattern and of material chosen by the housemother and girl together, with the interest and perhaps the assistance of the girl while it is being made) means much more than a beautifully fitted product from a central needleroom.

CHAPTER SIX

SEPARATENESS AND BELONGING

THE FAMILY IS the child's first community and it provides the setting in which he becomes a separate person. The family affords the child various kinds of experience: he learns that he has much in common with other members of the family, but that he also differs from them. The toleration by the other members of the family of his separate aims and activities frees him to develop along his own lines. In the larger community of the Home, with its greater complexity of relationships, it is important that the demands of organisation and conformity should not result in the individual's needs being overlooked.

Adult recognition of the child's vital need to be accepted as an individual who takes himself seriously, with a right to a private life of his own, can be strengthened by careful attention to certain features of life in a children's Home.

Private possessions

Studies of grown-up people, whether they be of two women working in a kitchen or of two men sharing a work bench, show that a sense of property and private possession is a deep-rooted human quality. Family life shows that growing maturity and deep common interests can help human beings to hold some property in common, and even to feel pride in common ownership. Nevertheless, it presents equally clear-cut, everyday examples of how difficult and even impossible common ownership of some things is. Perhaps most of the quarrels settled by parents are over borrowed playthings and borrowed clothing. Even in maturity sharing is difficult. There is always something of ourselves and our property which we reserve as our own, ultimately to be at our disposal and only to be given up if we wish it.

It is not surprising, therefore, that "my very own" should be a common phrase on the lips of children, nor is it surprising that they will go to great lengths to preserve something entirely for themselves.

The following was observed in an over-large nursery group:

Children secrete precious little objects down behind the skirting boards or up chimneys, in an endeavour to preserve them from the other children. I could not get any child to go to the lavatory or wash or go to the surgery until he had first been able to find an adult to hold and keep whatever small toy or tin he was playing with at the time. The pressure of the group on the children's sense of property is dismaying and the straits into which they are forced to "keep" or preserve their things is at once pathetic and frightening and the strain and anxiety during a single day must be immense.

Good Homes go to some pains to make it easy for the children to retain some personal belongings. It is widely realised that a child can have even more affection for an old, unhygienic-looking doll than an adult for an old pipe or armchair, and that children's queer collections of junk are as priceless as the oddments in a woman's work-basket or in a man's tool chest.

Here are old reports on pioneer Homes, which set the standards now universally accepted:

The Nursery staff realise the need for each child to have his individual possessions, and they have worked to provide a bag for each, in which he can keep whatever he likes. A special feature of this Nursery is the wall pocket in which each child keeps his individual treasures.

Each boy has a table and drawer beside his bed where he keeps his personal treasures, not clothes or slippers, but a few conkers, an old match box, a book and a penknife as well as oddments that can only be classed as junk.

Personal possessions and a little pocket money, as well as helping to teach respect for the feelings of others, may serve to make the child realise that he is of some importance.

After the provision of individual lockers in a hostel for difficult children, not only was there a marked drop in pilfering, but a general improvement within six months.

One of the children who had been brought up in an institution remarked with joy, "Now I have something of my own to give."

This self-respect is the basis of educability and social adjustment, and it is of enormous importance that by every means in our power each child should be helped to feel that he is of value to himself.

Private lockers and private correspondence

The establishment of a principle that private lockers should not be opened, even by members of the staff, marked one stage in the orientation of Homes towards the needs of childhood. But the child, certainly the child under about eleven years old, likes to share with adults, and the time comes in a well-integrated family Home when it would seem artificial for the housemother to ask permission to look in a child's locker, just as it would be artificial for a real mother to stand on such ceremony with her own child. Nevertheless, in an ordinary family a child's real wish for secrecy over some specific thing would be respected. This is well illustrated by children's attitudes to letters from home:

> In a reception Home for twenty-five boys and girls the children are free to write and receive letters from home without supervision. If a child is markedly reticent about these letters the staff will wonder why and will look out for signs that the child is worried about the contents. Properly approached, the child might welcome the chance to show what is in the letter. A letter left lying about is often a tacit invitation to the staff to discuss its contents and might well be taken up by saying to the child, "Would it help if I were to see this letter?"

Sharing

The staff of a Home will know that a child is certain of his right to possessions when he begins to want to share them with others. Little children have not reached the stage at which they can do this, and older children who have not had the opportunity to keep things all for themselves rarely reach a stage of heartfelt sharing either. This stage is reached spontaneously by most children in a good family atmosphere, provided the child's right not to share is first preserved for him long enough. Children cannot be made generous by enforced sharing, although they may, by this means, be made to feel the obligation to share.

Continuity of possession

The child's need for material things which symbolise for him his former life can be met in some small degree by allowing him to bring to the Home his own clothes and his most prized possessions.

As recently as 1950, *Brian*, a dull child aged four, was admitted to a local authority Nursery. Although he was known to have come from a clean and reputable home, the very first thing that the nurse did in the entrance hall was to strip him of all his clothes. She handed the clothes in a parcel to the child care officer and re-dressed Brian in nursery clothes. This was the routine procedure for all newly admitted children, rigidly carried out to avoid subsequent disputes with parents about allegedly lost or damaged clothing.

There are, of course, other ways of forestalling parental complaints. Nowadays, staff are careful not to do anything which would appear to the child to be derogatory of his family or of the grown-ups for whom he has an attachment. They make special efforts to see that every change is made as gradual and acceptable as possible, and recognise that clothes and possessions are the tangible link, and sometimes the only link, with the persons who cared for the child before admission. Toys and clothing, however disreputable, will be accepted at the child's own valuation.

Pocket money

The relatively large amount of pocket money given to children in Homes often surprises newcomers. In making comparison with the amounts given in private families it is well to remember that the child in a family receives a good deal in kind in addition to a small sum in cash. If he goes to the pictures with his parents they probably pay for him: they may give him extra money for Scout subscriptions and may buy him all kinds of non-essential oddments, such as extra pencils and rubbers for school. It is not so much the fixing of a standard rate-for-age that is needed as a careful adjustment in relation to the child's reasonable expenses. In any large-scale organisation there must be budgeting and the fixing in advance of a permitted limit to certain heads of expenditure. If a committee run a number of Homes they will naturally want to have some degree of uniformity between children of the same age, so that those in one Home are not worse off than those in another. It is therefore usual to lay down a fairly generous cash scale (which is known to the children) and to require them to finance all their recreational and non-essential expenditure out of it. Those in charge of the Home are usually allowed an additional sum for occasional organised outings and entertainments.

It is generally felt that children should be free to spend their pocket money as they please. It therefore follows that there need to be two separate heads of provision: a sum paid in cash and another sum at the

c

disposal of the houseparent to finance the kind of non-essential expenditure which is part of the fun between real parents and their children. Children can be encouraged to put aside a proportion of their pocket money for such regular calls as church collections and subscriptions to youth organisations and they can also be encouraged to save. The practice of saving is best related to short-term goals for younger children, such as saving up to have extra to spend on holiday or to buy a present for Mum, rather than the amassing of figures in a Post Office book. If the committee wish to give a regular weekly sum specifically for national savings, it might be best to keep this distinct in the child's mind from his free pocket money, for example, by giving it on the day that savings money is collected at school rather than in an inclusive pocket-money payment on Saturday.

The generosity of real parents may be governed by the fluctuating state of their own finances, and many a child has been told he must wait to the end of the week for some quite reasonable purchase. The provision of a fixed sum each week at the houseparents' disposal might reproduce for the child in a Home this feature of ordinary family life.

Presents

It is inevitable that some children in a Home will get more than others in the way of Christmas and birthday presents from outside. Some may be overwhelmed with presents from parents who feel deeply the loss of their children. Generally, the people in charge are given a total sum to spend as they wish on presents, and they will naturally allocate the expenditure according to each child's needs and not on a uniform basis. In doing this they will take into account what the child is getting from elsewhere. They will also find that suitable presents for older children cost a good deal more than those for younger ones, so that the expense rises steeply with the average age of the children. The fixing of a standard sum for an impersonal present "from the committee" to each child has therefore largely been abandoned.

Presents have, of course, much more significance than their intrinsic value. The most appreciated present may be quite inexpensive and may outwardly seem inadequate or even unsuitable. If it is a token of affection or even an earnest of a parent's existence and interest, the cheapest Christmas card may be more treasured than the most expensive toy.

Jean, aged fourteen, had lost her mother and had been rejected by her father for stealing. The father declined to write to her or visit, although he lived near. He was persuaded, however, to send a Christmas card. He did not think to write anything on the card, so Jean herself wrote inside "To Jean, with love from Daddy" before it was placed on the mantelpiece alongside the other children's cards.

What follows may seem petty in the extreme. It must, however, be remembered that every item of expenditure in some local authority children's Homes has to be separately accounted for and this raises problems for members of the staff in the giving of even small presents for children.

Each child in a Home will expect a Christmas and birthday present from the grown-ups he is living with: most of the children will have been saving up to give presents to the grown-ups too. One of the advantages of the small Home is that the numbers are sufficiently small for the houseparents to buy presents out of their own pockets without undue strain. But it would be unreasonable to expect this in larger Homes and a certain artificiality must creep into any plans made to finance the staff's expenditure on presents. It might be possible to meet the difficulty by giving a small expense allowance, though some would deprecate this. The provision of Christmas and birthday cards can be a substantial item in a large Home, but there is less difficulty here, since the essence of such tokens is the remembering and the careful choosing, and the actual cost of a personal card from a staff member might be taken without compunction from petty cash.

Homes which have been established for a long time often receive gifts from charitably minded organisations and individuals and from the proceeds of Church Christmas Tree Services and the like. More than half the fun of a present is lost if it comes anonymously. One of the saddest things which can happen to a visitor to a Home on Christmas Day is to have a child show the presents he has received and then to realise that the people from whom the presents came are strangers to the child. The most constructive form of help from kind people who do not know the children really well is to give cash to the houseparents, with the specific injunction that it is to be used freely to supplement their own expenditure on the children. Similarly the committee might provide an informal expense account as has been suggested above, and presents from the committee may then become a thing of the past.

Pets

Keeping pets has been recognised by Heads of children's Homes for many years as one of the ways of compensating children a little for some things which they lost when they had to leave their own families. Pets are an additional type of possession and one which calls out the protective qualities in the child. There is no risk of their being put away in a cupboard like inanimate toys. They provide an opportunity for sharing enjoyment and interest and responsibility with adults.

Different people have different ways of trying to make up for feelings of loneliness. A pet (unless it is a dog) is not necessarily company, but at least it is something of your own. What the lonely child misses is someone who specially belongs to him to give comfort and care. It is generally a hopeful sign if the lonely child, instead of getting depressed or aggressive, gives to a pet the mothering he wants for himself; and many a child who, in his isolation, has turned to excessive masturbation has been helped by being given an animal which he can tend and play with. It does not follow, of course, that every child who keeps a tame rabbit is compensating in this way.

Some children are preoccupied with larger animals, perhaps to an inordinate degree. It is unlikely that they will be greatly helped by being given such animals as pets, or by being allowed to ride or tend them. Large animals of strength or agility may fill a child's mind because they seem to him to be so powerful, whereas he himself feels small and weak in a shifting world of unreliable parent figures. It is as if he expected the animal to be on his side, helping him to cope with life. If he is actually faced with responsibility for looking after the animal his daydream may be shattered, and those who afford him the opportunity may be disappointed that it has not helped. The adults concerned will then learn what the child partly knew all along: that the child cannot look after anything, not even himself and his possessions.

The following incident illustrates the use that a child may seek to make of an animal at a critical moment:

Pamela, aged eleven, showed an inordinate interest in horses. She had been given a few opportunities to ride, but a holiday with a family who kept horses was abruptly terminated by her unruliness. She kept a scrapbook of horse pictures and had a phantasy horse which she tied to the bed post with a real halter every night. Sometimes in her phantasy she was a horse, she cantered and snorted like one, she put the halter on herself and put hay in her bed to eat. The extent of her phantasy life marked her out as a very disturbed child.

About a fortnight before Pamela was to meet her real mother for the first time in years, the child care officer (who had spent many visits to the Home getting to know Pam) told her about finding her mother and of her mother's readiness to meet her. It was explained that mother lived miles away in London and that the child care officer would take her on a two-day visit as soon as the school holidays started. The officer explained Pam's mother's circumstances and tried to help her to see why her mother had not been able to look after her, and why she still could not do so.

The next morning Pam disappeared before breakfast after telling another girl she was going to see her mother in London. The child care officer reports:

"The Matron of the children's Home telephoned to say that Pam's school clothes were still on her chair: her jodphurs, sweater and riding whip were missing. I set out in my car for the Home and on the way I saw Pam riding a horse towards me along the High Street. I waved and shouted, but she took no notice, so I turned round, overtook her and stopped. Pam saw me, but rode past, so I chased her again and drove alongside, talking to her through the open nearside window. After a bit I persuaded her to stop and dismount. Pam was now very subdued, with tears streaming down her face and a teddy bear tucked in her jodphurs. She refused to come into the police station, so a policewoman came to see Pam at the Home later in the day. Pam said she had not taken the horse to ride to London to see her mother. She claimed that she had just wanted to get away from the children's Home because all the other children were 'on to her'. It must have taken a lot of nerve to go into the riding stables and ride away with a strange horse. Before setting out Pam had ridden the horse down the shallow steps and taken him for a gallop along the sands and up the steps again: the hoof marks were still there to prove her story. It was hard to imagine that the sad-eyed tight-lipped child who had sat in my car was the same one who had set out an hour earlier on this escapade."

The real horse was no substitute for the phantasy. Pam had told her friend she was going to see her mother in London. In finding her way to a horse instead she revealed that what she was preoccupied with was a strong exciting creature which could give her freedom and happiness: in short, the Mother of her dreams. The episode was probably precipitated by her anxieties that the mother she was going to meet shortly would be less satisfying than the mother of her dreams. After the first few miles Pam was secretly relieved to be rescued by the child care officer. It would be no solution to provide Pam with a horse of her own, and she is just as well served by her collection of pictures and books. (In fact Pam was later sent to a private boarding school where horses were kept, but there was no noticeable release of emotional tension.)

To return to the smaller animals like rabbits, guinea-pigs and hamsters which feature so largely in children's Homes; it is worth considering whether these serve the function for which they are supposedly intended—namely, to give the children something more to love and care for. That they do not care for them is often the cause of friction between children and housemother, who may eventually conclude that keeping pets serves no good purpose. While it is true that they scarcely serve the purpose for which they were provided, it cannot be overlooked that they serve another very definite purpose. They reproduce, have babies, feed and suckle them and manifest an intricate family life at a level which is of great interest to the children. The staff can use this opportunity to make contact with the children about reproduction and birth, the divergent roles of the parents and their functions in the little families. In this way the animal families focus the children's phantasies but, unlike Pamela's horse, they offer an opportunity to bring these phantasies face-to-face with realistic instruction and discussion.

Organising a Home to provide for possessions and pets

Every matron knows how much allowing a child to have personal possessions adds to the difficulty of running a Home and keeping it reasonably tidy and clean. It is not surprising that the very limited staff of the older large Homes were obliged to discourage the hoarding of possessions and that periodical purges of "rubbish" from the children's private lockers were carried out. In the model plans for small Homes put out by the Home Office, immediately after the Children Act was passed, there was provision for a "hobbies room". Some authorities who have built these hobbies rooms on to their Homes have found them very little used. A workshop in the garden or a work bench in the garage is one thing, but a room set aside in the house for the practice of hobbies is quite another. Children in ordinary families want to keep their possessions handy around them in the living-room along with the books and comics and mother's sewing basket and father's pipes and newspapers. There is no short cut to overcoming the disorder which must follow from a very large family sharing one or two living-rooms. The secret of success is having adequate staff in the Home so that they have the time and patience to take notice of each child's interests and to ensure that their impedimenta are kept in reasonable order.

It is opportune to comment both on the highly regimented Home in which activity may be severely restricted and the markedly undisciplined Home in which "everything goes".

Order and tidiness

Anyone who has had to do with the supervision of older boys and girls after they have left a Home and gone out to live in lodgings or a foster home will know that the orderly upbringing of institutional life is no guarantee whatever that the practice of tidiness will persist in adolescent and adult life. Some of the most revolting self-made slums are made by mothers and fathers who were themselves brought up in conditions of rigid orderliness. Of course this is not true of all Homes children. Some of them become slovenly, some behave ordinarily and some turn out obsessionally tidy. But the incidence of really marked disorderliness amongst institutionalised children is too noticeable to be discounted as fortuitous. This is not to say that the régime of a children's Home produces adult disorder, but simply that it does not follow that lasting "habits of tidiness" will be inculcated by a tidy upbringing.

There are three factors which make for undue emphasis on order in a children's Home.

First, a lot of people are sharing a confined living space; these people are *children* with a diversity of activities and interests and a preoccupation with material things; and there are not enough bedrooms for each to have a room of his own to which his muddles can be confined. The remedy for this is smaller numbers, more space for each person, smaller bedrooms, plenty of cupboards, and places like cycle sheds and home workshops where juvenile occupations can be peaceably pursued.

Secondly, there is a world-wide desire of the human race to make an impression upon the stranger who comes into a dwelling-place. There can be few housewives who do not make at least a quick tour of the premises to fold up the newspapers and pat the cushions before a visitor is expected. To some the prospect of strangers entering the home is well-nigh intolerable. Now a children's Home lies under the constant threat of unannounced visitation. Any one of dozens of committee members and councillors may feel he has the right or even the duty to visit. Then there are local public personages who may want to take a kindly interest. The doctor and the parson, the teacher and the nurse will perforce come more often than they would to a private dwelling. The council's auditors, sanitary inspectors, building surveyors and fire protection officers all have responsibilities to the Home. Parents visit, often with a hostile and critical eye ready to observe and to complain about any supposed irregularity. Child care officers have business in the Home and senior officers of the children's department have a special responsibility to ensure that things are in order. Lastly, there are the Home Office Inspectors, whose function is wider and more constructive than their title suggests, but who cannot divest themselves of the inspectorial role.

Thirdly, there is the widespread belief, already referred to, that children (particularly other people's children) should be brought up in a tidy environment in order to inculcate habits of tidiness. This was exemplified by the new committee member who carried out a statutory visit to a children's Home and who, being invited to put his name and comments in the visitors' book, wrote, "Visited today and found everything clean and tidy."

The combined effect of all these pressures is to force practically every houseparent into maintaining a degree of order which is excessive compared with the conditions in the generality of private houses. Anything which we, and all the visitors referred to above, can do to relieve the tension will make a positive contribution, not only to the homeliness of the Home, but to the emotional tone of the household.

In children's Homes the see-saw of fashion between the desire for tidiness and the tolerance of disorder has remained heavily weighted on the side of tidiness for several generations. Considering all the pressure that is put on the staff of Homes to present an impeccable interior to visitors, it seems unlikely that there will be any dramatic change in the near future, although there has been a tendency towards more homeliness in the last few years. This tendency has come about partly because of better provision of staff, space and furnishings and partly because of a growing swing away from institutional ideas. It remains true, however, that only a certain kind of housewife can be happy in the surroundings which are still expected to be a feature of children's Homes and that recruitment to residential work is impoverished because many loving and mature people would not be prepared to make their home under the supposedly censorious eyes of so many official visitors. This is one of the many factors which contribute to the wide gulf which still exists between the best of children's Homes and any ordinarily good foster home.

Care in a disordered household as a remedy

The universal tidiness of local authority children's Homes has led some child guidance experts to search about for people who will take exceptional children into their homes and bring them up in a different setting. It is argued that some older children need to live through infantile experiences and that they are helped to do this by being in a household where extremes of disorder are tolerated. When this method of treatment is embarked upon it is important that the situation should be under the skilled control of the psychiatric advisers who have prescribed the treatment. Furthermore, the quality of the child's emotional needs and his social circumstances must be kept constantly under review. It is not enough simply to hand over the care of the child to people who will let him regress. There must be parallel work with the child's own family or foster family to whom he will ultimately return. The difficulty about exceptional people who can tolerate infantile behaviour from an older child is that they themselves are often in an infantile stage of development: their own bedrooms are in no better state of cleanliness and decency than the state to which the child reduces his. What we are looking for, and what we are unlikely to find outside the children's ward of a mental hospital, are people who will allow the child to regress because they understand him and love him, without being people whose own behaviour is perpetually on a par with that of the child whose disorder they are trying to cure. In spite of the child's disorder the régime itself needs to be a stable, secure and loving one in which the child's needs are confidently being met. What destroys the value of some of these exceptional households is that the laxity spills over into all facets of the child's care: the adults in charge are careless about leaving the children unattended, the food is insufficient, the cooking poor and the meals late: the child is loved when he is there, but when he leaves them, even for a holiday, they do not write to him or send his clean clothes or the prized possession which was inadvertently left behind.

The child does not always react against this implied lack of affection. For the sake of the tolerance which relieves certain tensions in him he may be ready to accept serious deficiencies in the day-to-day care and interest shown in him. He exchanges one set of disturbing factors in his life for another set. This may or may not be a help to him in the long run.

What so often goes with this particular kind of immaturity in adults is the sense that other people, children and adults alike, exist to be used.

The visitor is welcomed not as someone whose company is desired for its own sake but as someone who is to be sucked into the maelstrom of misbehaviour. They have abandoned their civilised standards and they demand that the visitor shall do the same. When the stranger is accepting, they will at that moment give him all they have got and expect the same in return. The household is a little fortress of disorder which seeks to make allies amongst the outside world, but only on its own terms, which include recognition of its complete autonomy. There is no room for sharing responsibility for children or for sharing their affection. The kind of person who has no desire for cleanliness and comfort in his living conditions is able to point out that he is getting nothing for himself out of looking after maladjusted children and he therefore expects that those responsible for placing the child will recognise this show of altruism and give him a free hand. Whereas a controlled return to infantile behaviour may be recommended for a limited time, the attitude of the person who can tolerate this in his own home is likely to be "all or nothing": he wants the child to share his way of life for keeps or not at all. Such an attitude in adults is one kind of defence against life itself. When the grown-ups' personal need for acute disorder is so great, there is a risk that the situation may become intolerable to society, so that they live under the constant fear of action by the police or by the N.S.P.C.C. to remove the children under a magistrate's order to a place of safety. The risk of precipitate removal is a factor to be weighed before the child is placed. Nevertheless, an arrangement like this may be, for the very exceptional child, the best that can be done at the time. Too little is yet known about the ultimate effects in individual instances, and that little is by no means reassuring.

A feature of providing an assortment of possessions and activities in a children's Home is not only that organisation is difficult to maintain and some measure of disorder ensues. If children have an adequate supply of possessions they have additional means to wreak some of their destructiveness on those possessions. When this grows disproportionately, it becomes a major offence to any adult. It also becomes a feature of the economy of the Home. A short discussion of children's destructiveness is appropriate here.

Destructiveness

Complaints about destructiveness are not confined to younger children. Amongst older children it can often be traced in part to lack of supervision due to shortage of staff. But basically it is because of lack of understanding of the importance of occupation. *Destructiveness is most often a reaction to the disadvantages of institutional as compared with family life.* Many of these disadvantages have already been noted. To the extent to which a Home can take over the functions of a family, abnormal destructiveness will cease to occur, but there are causes of destructiveness which affect even the child in his own family. A measure of destructiveness is a normal childish attitude, which is not altered by the simple device of not providing anything to destroy.

Children, like adults, need to be able to reject or turn down what is offered to them. Sometimes that is the only way they can feel "right" about it. Every child loses or destroys his own possessions at some time or another. Often, this is the only way he can feel he owns them. Where nearly all possessions are communal, children frequently feel that destruction is the only way of asserting their rights to them.

Abnormal children, on the other hand, who apparently accept the communal life in its entirety, often do so at the expense of their emotional life. One child, whose history gave him every cause to be vindictive and bitter, produced no resentment, only the apathetic reaction, "I don't bother", to everything offered him. In this case, destructiveness would have been relatively normal: resignation only led him away from life. Having possessions, and if need be destroying them, has to precede effective education in protection and caring for your own things.

Destructive situations can also arise where the adult gives too much or where he unduly restricts the conditions in which things can be used. There is then no scope for the child to improvise. While generous provision for children is to be commended, not all their time should be spent in a sheltered and well-equipped environment. They should have the fun of "making do" and the salutary experience of doing without something unless they can achieve it by their own efforts. The paradox is that sometimes Homes children have their material wants too readily supplied while their inner needs are starved.

Destructiveness in phases of transition

It is disheartening to provide children with beautiful clothes and lavish accommodation and equipment, only to find that they do not look after these things or use them properly. This kind of behaviour often marks a child's transition away from a stage of dependency. There are two specially marked periods of change towards independence. One is the phase when the infant has found his feet in the new world of school and play outside his home and the other is the similar process in adolescence when most youths leave school and go out to the working life of adulthood. At both these stages the youngster garners his energy into his private world to which parents are only admitted on sufferance. Ask the fifteen-year-old where he is going and he will say, "Just going out." Ask the seven-year-old where he has been and he will say, "Just down in the wood: we saw a rabbit there." But neither will reveal the intense interest which has gone into his private thoughts or into his talks with friends of the same age.

At these times it is specially important to the child to possess himself. He needs to feel that his body and his clothes belong to him. To feel that one's own is one's own is basic to self-esteem and independence. At these times of transition the child may come to feel that his body as well as his clothes belong not to him but to his parents. In using his body and his clothes as weapons to further his rebelliousness against his parents he may appear to be seriously neglectful and destructive. The right course for the parent or houseparent caught up in this situation is a difficult one to steer. On the one hand we do not want to leave the child to his own devices, as if we did not care how dirty or disreputable he looks. On the other hand we do not want to press him so hard that he feels himself to be possessed: this feeling can reach depths of intensity which manifest themselves in symptoms such as accident-proneness.

Matron was very concerned because *Roger*, aged sixteen, attending the Technical College, left his single bedroom in such a muddle, with his clothes strewn all over the place. She let him see that she was afraid that a committee member would see the state of his room, but did not order him to clear it up. Instead she commented on the orderly way in which he kept his college note books and told visitors how much she relied on Roger to help her make up the accounts at the end of the month. When a tour of inspection was due Roger made a special effort to make his room tolerably presentable. Then Matron let him have a key to lock his bedroom up during the day, on condition he left the key where she could find it. She told him she would not look into his room without telling him.

The adolescent who stays in full-time education, or who undertakes an apprenticeship at a low wage, is under a special difficulty, because he cannot so easily keep his inner life private. He will have to ask for the special kinds of clothes which he feels express his personality. Residential staff often have to press the administrators and the committee very hard to get adequate clothing allowances and pocket money for some of their teenagers who are working on a low wage alongside other young people who are treated generously by their own parents. The situation is complicated because there may be other children of the same age in the Home who do not manifest the same tastes.

The traditional idea that young people should be discouraged from preoccupation with their appearance is not a helpful guide to the handling of those who are in a state of conflict over growing up.

June, just leaving school at fifteen, adopted a beatnik hairstyle and wanted to go out with another girl on Sunday afternoon in black stockings and a dirty duffle coat. Matron asked her to go out the back way and not let herself be seen in the residential part of the town, a condition which June readily accepted. Later, when June's child care officer called, Matron commented in June's presence what a nice figure the girl had and asked the child care officer to exercise special care in choosing some outdoor clothes for June, "because she pays for dressing and always takes a lot of trouble over her appearance".

The child care officer thought at first that this kind of treatment would make June vain, but, on getting to know her better, she realised that June benefited from open appreciation of her attractiveness.

The limits to belonging

This chapter ends by re-emphasising that belonging to a family is not an end in itself: the end is to strike a sound balance for each child between his need for separateness and his need for belonging. It is noticeable that some children who have had a reputation for aggressiveness or for moroseness in highly organised Homes have gone easily into foster homes or into lodgings and have ceased to display these symptoms. The child should have some freedom to choose whether or not he wants to take part in various kinds of activity, and further he should be able to try out various things and then discard them if they are not to his liking. Much of the process of growing up consists of this kind of trial and selection.

In the same way, the grown-ups themselves differ in their capacity for integration into the neighbourhood and the Head of each Home cannot be expected to conform to a pattern. Not every superintendent will want to join the Rotary Club: some will take a big part in organised social life and others will be more at home in making individual contacts in the pub, the football club or the British Legion. In this way they exemplify, in adult life, the principles that we are seeking to apply to the children. Each has his separate part to play: Johnny is always on the fringe when it comes to party games at Christmas, but it is he who makes the pictures to put round the walls as part of the decorations: Mary feels out of place on the concert stage and she prefers to be the one who prints the programmes.

CHAPTER SEVEN

OCCUPATIONS AND ACTIVITIES

THE LAST CHAPTER emphasised the child's need to be a separate person and tried to show how this can be made compatible with membership of a group. When a child's behaviour is not compatible with easy living in the group, it probably has some temporary or permanent significance for him. He needs to be helped towards a better adjustment to the demands of the others in the Home. We now go on to consider how the sharing of activities with adults can be used to further this growing-up process.

Sharing tasks with grown-ups

Family feeling in a Home can be fostered by the sharing of household tasks. In this way the child learns from the grown-up and also tends to become like the grown-up. He takes the first steps to becoming like an adult, not only in practical ways but in his wider ambitions. The process of sharing makes many practical difficulties for the staff. Only those with training and insight are likely to be prepared to overcome the difficulties for the sake of the homeliness that ensues. At one time quite young children were required to undertake a great burden of household work, because domestic help was not provided. Moreover, to make the routine easier this work was often not varied, the same child having to do exactly the same household task month after month. With the provision of adequate staff there came a swing away from participation by the children and some staff felt they might be criticised if the children were observed by visitors to be working. It was also found to be generally easier to do everything oneself rather than to let the children perform the lighter tasks. For example, one very over-worked matron was forced to exclude the children rigidly from the kitchen so that she could press on with a continuous round of cooking and washing-up, and another would not let secondary school children clean their own shoes because they got so messy.

Here by contrast, are reports on four other Homes:

Eight children of school age. The eldest girl came in from school and was welcomed, "Eva, I've been waiting for you. Now we can have tea laid if you'll help." While laying the tea, the children talked about the china and the cutlery and compared it with what they had in their own homes. Obviously, sharing in the task, which they may have done at home, revived memories for all of them.

Boys aged seven to fourteen. Warden and boys keep the garden and rockery in good order. The boys know all the names of the rock plants and tell you proudly. They keep hens and they mend the paths. The warden always works about with them, seldom leaving them to work alone, or at least without some interest from him.

Girls up to fifteen. The older girls sleep three or four to a bedroom. They love turning out the rooms and also turning round the furniture. "One week the wardrobe is here and another week there, but I don't mind."

A Residential Nursery. The cook is engaged on the understanding that she will have children into the kitchen, either singly or in small groups, to watch the cooking and do "pastry" play from time to time. Three times a week a selection of vegetables is sent to the group rooms and prepared for lunch by the children and group mothers. The children dust and polish tables and brass work in their own rooms and occasionally help do the small "blouse" wash which each group mother does at the end of the day.

Here are two matrons who had different slants on the same problem:

"I hoped the girls would be able to help in the house, but you have to be after them all the time. They won't work."

"The girls work very well if you work with them. After all, it's company they need. There's quite a lot of rivalry to do well while I'm about."

Participation by children can be extended to outdoor activities:

Home for twenty children. Mr. W. and the boys have built two swings, one for older and one for younger children, a pulley contraption between two trees whereby a basket swings on a cable from one tree to the other in the way a river crossing is sometimes done, and also a roundabout for young children. At the far end of the grounds, they have built a permanent tin camp with its own latrines, where in the summer boys can live, camping out. The girls have bell tents in other parts of the grounds, cook outside, and sleep out. The boys work in the garden—Mr. W. with them—he gets into old clothes for the occasion. He is very knowledgeable on gardens, and lets them share his interest in pruning, manuring, hot-house cultivation and kitchen gardening. They keep rabbits and breed them for eating. They have a racing track where the boys run races with small motor-cars for small money prizes.

Of course there is a danger of this kind of thing becoming an end in itself or tending to give the Home special features which make it a show-place for the edification of visitors. Staff who are only concerned with the interests of the children will always be ready to abandon a project when the children have had enough of it. They will have equal warmth for those children who do not want to take part in organised activity and who prefer more solitary pursuits. Committees and administrators can do a good deal to encourage these projects and can be thankful for the delight which many housefathers get from helping the children in boyish pursuits. They can generally be assured that the women in the household will keep the scheme in its proper perspective.

Belonging to the neighbourhood

Access to community life, which is open to the child with a family, used sometimes, for various reasons, to be withheld from the Homes child. One of the handicaps which made it so difficult for children evacuated from Homes during the war to go into billets was that, having had so little experience of private living, they proved unable to avail themselves of the opportunity of foster homes which the evacuation scheme offered. A survey of one group of hostels showed that, out of eighty-nine children who had proved "unbilletable" thirty-eight had lived before the war in local authority Homes.

The original plan was that children who had lived in wartime residential nurseries should be billeted privately on reaching the age of five years. During the third year of the war it became increasingly obvious that residential nursery children were less suitable for billeting. Billet mothers complained of the children's habits and their inability to fit into family life, and their "out-of-placeness" in the village. This complaint was so widespread that the Ministry of Health authorised the setting up of special hostels for ex-nursery children between the ages of five and seven. This clearly indicated both the resentment which small children do not hesitate to express at changing their homes, and the failure of the nurseries to adjust them to normal living.

The following is a comment by the Chief Boarding-out Officer of Dr. Barnardo's at the time:

"Some children, who have been in institutions for some time, find it difficult to adjust to freedom and responsibility in home life. This has been borne out by the experiences of evacuation of children from Public Assistance Institutions, where they have lived for so long that, when they were in an ordinary home, they had no means of knowing where freedom ended and responsibility began."

Why had these institutions been so unsuccessful?

Analysis of the situation of individual Homes showed a variety of reasons for failure to mix with the community. All too often the community resented the existence of children's Homes in their midst. Sometimes this resentment was traceable to local snobbery; the Home had intruded into a good residential area. There were fears (generally unfounded) that gardens and grounds would not be kept up to the local standard and that property prices might deteriorate. Fears of the children's behaviour had preceded their taking up residence and were based on differences in class standards. Sometimes, the feeling was rooted in the not unjustifiable mistrust that greets any large group of children arriving anywhere, until they have proved themselves reliable neighbours. Often particular incidents gave colour to the popular resentment. Every local authority Home that is not patently a Nursery gets dubbed "Remand Home" at first (not that Remand Homes are notably unsuccessful in getting integrated into community life, but it takes rather longer). The growth of confidence is not helped when a Home is used as a place of safety or a reception Home for children sent by the Courts. Although there are strict rules against publishing addresses in Juvenile Court cases, in a small town everyone knows when a child is sent to a Home.

Large groups of Homes, built on one estate, have a special difficulty. The very numbers of workers and children may set up barriers which, with the best will on the part of workers and of the outside community, it may be hard to break down. That the children suffer if some solution is not found is very clear. They feel out of place in normal social situations and their consequent bizarre behaviour invites and provokes distrust in others, unless they are under constant supervision.

Children from a residential school for girls and small boys, which is extremely well controlled and sheltered, seemed afraid when they attended a Christmas party where other children were being noisy and spirited.

The children from X . . . a well controlled Home, tended to behave well individually outside the Home, but sometimes to indulge in gang activities of a delinquent kind. It was as if they were afraid when alone, and felt their only way to meet normal people was "in force" or aggressively.

Initial hostility and prejudice against the opening of children's Homes is still apparent in some areas. Of late years, with better trained staff and a better ratio of staff to children, it has been possible to put more time and effort into integrating the Home into the community. So that, whereas a Home is still rarely welcomed at the outset, it does not generally take long for it to be accepted and even regarded as an amenity. In one market town, where the children's part in school and youth organisations, in sport and in the church choir was especially valued, every project to close the Home has met with vigorous protest from the neighbourhood.

It may be useful to study some ways in which this happy situation may be brought about.

Making a contribution to the neighbourhood

Barriers to neighbourliness can become formidable or can disappear according to the steps that are taken to deal with them. They are stronger, but not less removable than, community oppositions which meet particular families. The staff of Homes can take steps to bring the community in touch with themselves and with the children. Those with easy personal contacts and wide interests can organise activities which add something to community life. A good warden of a large Home can organise plays, parties and lectures and make the Home their centre, so that people know the inside of the Home as well as they know their other neighbours' houses. Distrust is allayed and a working basis established for the children's acceptance in true neighbourliness.

In one Home for twenty-five boys, the staff and boys have their own orchestra and contribute to outside entertainment in the village. Once a month, the Home gives a dance to which girls from local Homes and families are invited.

The Matron of one Residential Nursery often invites the local W.E.A. group for meetings. Neighbouring school staffs also attend the staff's training lectures. In this way many contacts are made and opportunities opened up for the children to visit outside the Nursery.

This sort of activity is suitable for large Homes and Nurseries, rather than for family Homes, but in any case the aim is not to make the Home into a Community Centre, but simply to ensure that it contributes its share to local social life, in the same way as any large outward-looking family does. Some of the activities may be specifically for grown-ups in the same way as parents will sometimes entertain their grown-up friends, the children taking a back seat for the evening. Then Matron can say to the children next week, "It's your turn now." The delicate balance between child-centredness and adult-centredness sometimes becomes upset in one direction or the other, and it has to be carefully poised.

In one family Home for eight children, Matron is treasurer of the Townswomen's Guild, and committee meetings are held in rotation in the committee members' houses. When it is her turn the children set the room ready and hand round the refreshments at the beginning of the meeting. Then they know they are expected to put themselves to bed rather earlier than usual and not interrupt the committee meeting. Some of the committee members visit the Home on other occasions, bringing their husbands and children, and also invite the children to their own homes.

One of the artificial features of life in a Home used to be that it was too much centred round the activities of the children, so that they did not get any understanding of adult ways. The staff tended to give the impression that home life was organised solely for the children's benefit and they took their own recreation in separate private apartments or outside the Home altogether.

More reticent wardens may reach the same goal by having a few close personal contacts which eventually bridge the children's way to the community. Soon after one Home for ten children was opened a neighbour wrote to the Town Hall expressing disgust that the children were taken to school by car. The staff did not show resentment at this. Instead, the matron's husband wrote to the complainants explaining that he went to work in his car every day and that he dropped the children near school on his way to town, just as many other parents in the vicinity did. He ended his letter with an invitation to come to the Home and meet the children. When there was no response he called on the neighbour with an invitation to tea, which was accepted. In return, one or two of the Home's children were invited back to see television. Some months later, while the matron and her husband were on holiday, the children got up to mischief and caused a small road roller to run away. By then the standing of the Home in the neighbourhood was such that this incident did not cause any undue upsurge of public opinion against the children.

Explaining the Home to the neighbourhood

Staff of Homes and child care officers may be invited to address local groups of rotarians, women's institutes and the like. At such meetings they will often be asked how people can help the Home. The traditional response used to be to get up a collection to give the children a party in the Home or the parish hall, or to provide toys at Christmas. By means of question and answer at a meeting it is possible to modify this approach so that people understand it is not organised charity but ordinary neighbourliness which is most appreciated. It is the more effective if the speaker is able to illustrate stories of actual neighbourly relationships which are known to him.

We do not underestimate the qualities of personality and the degree of effort from which successful relationships result. A warden who is unduly reticent or overworked or lacking in self-confidence may make capital out of initial opposition. His own resentment gives colour to local suspicion and his efforts to defend his position by formalising the children's relations outside the house set up a vicious circle which is hopelessly at variance with the children's needs. There is then a risk that the staff who have no local social contacts will live for their "days off". They will feel that their two free hours daily are "no good" to them, as "what can they do with them?".

The community, too, sometimes covers its sense of its own shortcomings by the comment that the staff are self-sufficient, if the Home is a large one. A certain degree of isolation is inevitable at first because, unlike the teacher, the warden deals with "foreign" children, so that his vocational links with his neighbours may be comparatively few. If he is a person with considerable social feeling, he is that much better equipped for his job. Unless he has been trained to realise the importance of contacts for himself and the children, he may too easily be content with placating his neighbours by ensuring that the children's conduct is faultless. Because it is known that children are sometimes sent to Homes for behaviour problems, people tend to be surprised if the children do not behave boisterously when they are out on social visits. The pleased and surprised comments which are then made may put an unwholesome pressure on the staff to try to maintain an unnatural decorum. The neighbours need to be helped to understand that it is not bad table manners and the omission to say "Thank you for having me" which lead children into Homes, but much less obvious and more serious difficulties. The growth of such understanding can be rewarding to everybody.

Belonging to the Church

Fruitful access to the community often lies through the Church and the school.

> *Home for twenty-five children aged eight to twelve.* A newly set up Home ascribed its good relations with the neighbourhood to the welcome given by the Vicar, who invited the children to tea in batches and allowed them to use his field and spent an evening a week in their playroom.

> *Home for eight boys aged seven to thirteen.* The newly married curate has no children of his own as yet. He very frequently visits this Home which has a single woman in charge. He plays cricket with the boys in the garden and takes them for walks. He knows all about the boys' families and about their hobbies. He helps them with handicrafts in the winter evenings and helps the younger boys with their letters home. Of course, the boys take part in all the Church activities appropriate to their age. When Matron was on leave one of the boys got into trouble with the police. The other seven boys in a body hustled him off to the Church to seek the help of the curate.

> *Home for ten boys and girls.* At one time all the children who were not Roman Catholics were sent off to the parish church regardless of their religious affiliations. When a new boy who was a Baptist was admitted, the Warden consulted the local Baptist Superintendent Minister. As there was no Baptist church in the town, the boy was commended to another non-conformist denomination. This was the first time that members of this chapel had had any links with the children's Home. Arrangements were made for older children to collect the boy and take him to the services. Members of the congregation invited him to tea and eventually he formed a firm relationship with a married couple with children of their own. He stays with them for some week-ends and for a week each holiday.

But the Church is not invariably an open door to the community. Elderly parsons of elderly flocks sometimes find difficulty in providing

for children at the ordinary services and lay people running
Sunday schools can find their talents unequal to managing groups
of children who may have had no previous contact with the
Church.

Home for children aged seven to fourteen. The Vicar complained when
we brought our children to Church, and refused to have the plate
passed to them. The children brought their pennies back and
commented most disappointedly.

This was not an isolated instance: similar examples have been given
by several Heads of Homes, but such situations can practically always be
modified by a careful approach to the parish priest.

Reception Home for twenty-five children. The Rector is a manager of
the primary school and he was instrumental in getting a resolution
passed pressing the committee to educate children inside the Reception Home because the continual coming and going and the disturbed behaviour of the children disrupted the running of the
school. He dissuaded the warden from sending children to his
Sunday school for fear his voluntary teachers would leave. He felt
it would be no help to the children to come to the ordinary service
as it was a fashionable neighbourhood and the sermons had to be of
an intellectual nature unsuited to children. When approached by the
Warden, however, the Rector readily undertook responsibility for
the Reception Home children and offered to send a curate to hold a
weekday service in the Home. This was accepted as a start, but it was
pointed out that our aim was to help the children to become an
accepted part of the parish community. The Rector then found a
lay-reader to run a children's service in church every Sunday for our
children and for those from one or two preparatory schools, as well
as for children from families in the parish.

Belonging to the school

Similarly, an individual approach to a Head Teacher may modify
the attitude of the school to children from the Home.

There had been several scattered Homes in the town since before
the first war. The teachers did their best for the children but they
adopted an attitude towards them which was different from that
which they displayed towards the other children. The Homes

children did not bring dinner money (which was paid centrally). A constant guerrilla warfare went on between the housemothers and the teachers over such things as sports kit, payment for woodwork and cookery products and "keeping in" after school. Homes staff were resistant if a teacher showed an interest in a particular child and were resentful of being "sent for" when a child misbehaved. The Homes children were specially examined by the school doctor every term and paraded in the hall or playground for this and other purposes. From time to time teachers complained to the education authority about having so many backward and difficult children from the Homes. After the Children Act the situation grew worse, the teachers questioning the vigorous policy of boarding-out and of restoration to parents. The children's committee met this in three ways. The number of children in the Homes was drastically reduced and several Homes were closed, new buildings being erected in different towns in the county. The Homes staff were encouraged to accompany each new child to school on his first day and to inform the Head Teacher of the child's history and family, and teachers were invited to take part in discussion about the children in the Homes. All this was reinforced by school visits from child care officers and from the educational psychologist employed by the children's committee. When special issues arose the children's officer visited the school. When a new Headmaster was appointed to the boys' secondary modern school, the management committee invited him to lunch with them in the one remaining Home. The Superintendent keeps in almost daily touch with the Headmaster by personal visits and by telephone. The Headmaster sometimes goes for walks with the Homes boys during the holidays and takes an interest in the sports and handicrafts which the Superintendent organises out of school hours. Neither the Superintendent nor the Headmaster has to rely on tales borne by the boys, because they have confidence in each other. Any potential misunderstanding is immediately cleared up by a telephone call.

Part-time employment

For children in their last year or so at school the possibility of part-time work within the reasonable limits permitted by law offers another avenue into the outside world and at the same time may help to establish on a more realistic basis the child's choice of a vocation. In the country the farmers and market gardeners are often pleased to offer a few hours' employment on Saturdays and at holiday times, and in the towns a warden may build up a connection with one or two garage-owners and shopkeepers who will give a handy boy or girl a trial. Properly handled the children will compete for the privilege of being allowed to take a part-time job, as much for the status and sense of growing up as for the remuneration it brings.

Youth clubs

Organised youth movements and clubs and team games of all kinds offer a chance to mix with other children in a less formal setting than school and church. It is here that the well-sited Home in a town has the advantage in that there will be a variety of organisations to suit varying tastes and to ensure that the children can be distributed in such a way that they do not form tight little gangs of Homes children within each organisation. This is another argument for small Homes of mixed ages in which the children will have a variety of recreational and educational needs which will be catered for in more than one youth organisation and more than one school. The enthusiasm of the committee or of the superintendent for one particular form of youth activity to the exclusion of others has both advantages and disadvantages. The eagerness of some children will be reinforced by the special interest of the staff but, on the other hand, all boys are not equally attracted by a movement such as the Scouts. Some youth groups tend to make considerable intellectual demands on their members. The backward child joining such a group may find the intellectual inferiority which frustrates him at school all day emphasised in his recreational activities as well. Heads of Homes should not be criticised for having less than a hundred per cent of their children in membership of youth organisations. There may be a proportion of children in the Home who are not ready to join any group and others who will never want to join, preferring to follow more individual pursuits.

"Aunties and Uncles"

Some Homes, especially large ones, still find it helpful to have a scheme for recruiting "Aunties and Uncles" and such Homes may also participate in the distribution of presents for "lonely children", which is made each Christmas by a Sunday newspaper. Those in charge of Homes will, of course, be most careful to assess the motives and the steadfastness of anyone wishing to befriend a child in a Home before any introduction is made. Much will depend upon the nature of the Home and the policy governing admissions and discharges to and from the Home. If the Home does not adopt a vigorous boarding-out policy and if the Home is remote from the families of the children in their care, it may well be that the formal introduction of a visitor will be to the child's advantage. If, however, as in many local authority Homes, the staff are working towards an early restoration to parents or an early placement in a foster home, the introduction of a visitor may unnecessarily complicate the child's relationships. With regard to the well-intentioned newspaper scheme, there are many Homes nowadays where none of the children could possibly be described as lonely and where extra Christmas presents would be less welcome than they would be to many less-affluent children living with their own parents.

Friends to tea

A superintendent of a Home was once instructed that each child in his Home should bring a friend home to tea and that a report should be presented the following month to say that this instruction had been complied with. The anxiety to put an end at once to the rigid exclusion of children from outside can be understood, and it is to be hoped that a more spontaneous relationship with schoolmates sprang from this sudden reversal of policy. For a child from outside to come as a visitor to a children's Home is rarely the same thing as visiting a private family. In a private house the whole family goes out of its way to make a visitor specially welcome, whereas the schoolchild visitor to a Home may be made to feel that he is entirely the responsibility of the child who introduced him. The Homes child may find that he is not invited back to his friend's house, for a variety of reasons peculiar to his being a child in a Home. The potential hostess may think that the Homes children are not allowed out, or she may not be anxious for her child to mix with children from a Home, or she may fear that the Homes child will take undue advantage of hospitality and outwear his welcome. An awareness of all these factors on the part of Homes staff may well overcome all the difficulties.

Occasionally a neighbour's child becomes attracted to a Home and spends a lot of time there. The child may be lonely at home, or he may have a parent who encourages him to stay out of doors. Sometimes such a child is younger than most of the children living in the Home and he may then be treated as a kind of mascot and be shown off to visitors, in front of the other children, as "this little boy who would rather live here than with his mummy and daddy". To listen to this unreal announcement must be a bitter experience for children who are prevented from living with their own mothers and fathers.

The personality of the staff as a factor in reaching out to the neighbourhood

If wardens go half-way towards meeting the community the results may be very worth while. In this respect a married couple, through the support they lend to each other, may more easily find a way through these difficulties. The possession of good social qualities and some measure of education must rank as important features in the selection of staff. Above all, the warden needs to understand the importance of the community to the child.

CHAPTER EIGHT

HELPING THE CHILD TO SELF-DISCIPLINE

WE HAVE DEVOTED considerable space to discussing ways in which the child's human need for warm and friendly companionship with adults receives satisfaction. It must have been clear throughout that we envisage not only providing gratifications for children's instinctual needs but that we have discussed this in a context where gratification and restraint go side by side. That the capacity for restraint matures from birth onwards, is one of the most striking factors about human development. Every mother is impressed when the random, impulsive actions of her baby first give place to a heedful recognition of her warnings and then to self-regulated activity.

It is important to understand something about the development of this capacity for restraint. People often say that children in Homes are so difficult and undisciplined that it is not practicable to apply to them the principles of child care which have been outlined in earlier chapters. Attempts to apply these principles may fail unless the need for developing restraint is understood and accepted.

Human character is based first on primitive instinctual needs and secondly on the growth, within the personality, of structures for ensuring restraint. These structures grow out of the child's need to protect himself. He learns very early that he will hurt himself if he acts purely on impulse.

One structure, the ego, has built up a body of experience which teaches the child that certain ways of proceeding are ineffective, or even self-damaging, and that other ways will bring him new experience and satisfaction. This process of self-protection by remembering and assimilating one's experience is lifelong. With the growth of the ego, children learn that some demands are too painful in their results and must be given up: others must be achieved in a safer and more realistic fashion. The capacity to restrain impulsive action has an importance transcending the need to guard against common dangers. It can lift life on to a totally new plane.

A child who has received loving care from his parents does not have to learn everything by bitter experience. He accepts the parents as his guides to reality. Then, because he loves and trusts them and enjoys their care, he will begin to care about himself as a person; loving and protecting himself as the parents love and protect him and taking pride in his own growth as they take pride in it. The function of "protecting" may lead to his caring for animals or for a garden. The idea of being a protecting, cherishing, person may even ultimately direct his choice of work in life. He may want to teach others, as he was taught; or look after their bodies, as his was looked after. This process of identification with the parents' rôle may determine his choice of interests as well as of behaviour.

Identification with the parents

It is not difficult for the grown-up to understand identification when the child adopts the parents' qualities out of love and admiration. A little girl becomes a "mummy" to her dolls and a little boy "drives" a car, because this is to be like the parents. But young children also identify out of anxiety and this process of identification, as a means of overcoming conflict and isolation, is a more difficult one to comprehend.

It is impossible for any parent to make the all-demanding baby feel that all his needs are instantly met. Every child must feel neglected from time to time and even unloved and unprotected. Fury because of this feeling of neglect may colour his feelings about his parents. At times the people whom he most loves and needs feel "bad" to him and this creates a conflict. Young children have one outstanding method of dealing with this conflict. They try to become like the parents in order to overcome the sense of isolation which conflict brings.

A child who has been frightened by the dentist will almost immediately "play dentists" with another child: frightened by a dog, he is most likely to play at being a dog and biting someone else. In the same way, if his parents make him anxious he does not necessarily ask for an explanation or even become cross. Instead, he identifies with their unwelcome actions or attitudes, which then become part of himself. This enables him to pass on to others the experience and behaviour which have upset him. Some of these identifications are transient: others become permanently embodied in the child's character. The "hard" child, for instance, is the child who feels, or has felt, the hardness of others.

Much of a child's indiscipline can arise from such unrealistic identifications. To take a simple example, a little girl who feels ousted by a new baby and who is not helped to understand her jealousy may throw all her dolls out of the window, thus passing on the neglect she feels. The same motive may lead a more disturbed child, perhaps one whose experiences have been even more alarming, to kill her pets. Identification may thus take place for reasons of hate as well as for reasons of love and admiration. In the life of the ordinary child there are many situations which fortify his feeling that he is loved and protected and also many in which he experiences his parents as unprotecting and hateful.

It should not, therefore, surprise us, in dealing with a child in a Home, to find two things: an inability to protect and look after himself and realise his potential, and an inability to judge what the grown-ups in the Home feel about him and take into account in his behaviour what the social results of his actions are likely to be. With his confidence in his parents' care and protection undermined, he becomes careless in protecting himself. He also approaches other adults with the expectation that they will not protect him. His capacity to look after himself, and to let us look after him, are both impaired. The distrust thus engendered makes it difficult to form a relationship with him and so causes him to become inaccessible to our influence.

Children also achieve their knowledge of right and wrong and their standards of behaviour by the same process of identification. In this way they build a further structure into their character, which we call conscience. This is partly taken from rules which the parents lay down for them and partly from their assimilation of the rules which they see the parents themselves obey. Of course, even in a normal family, a child's standards may become confused if what is enjoined on him contrasts too sharply with the parents' own behaviour. Many children come into care with a long-standing conflict of this type. The very fact of the break-up of the family, even temporarily, implies parental inadequacy to the child. In these circumstances of frustration, disappointment and rage, and because of his immaturity, the child is scarcely ever able to make a sound judgment in the many factors— social, economic and personal—which have caused his parents to make this decision. All too often, his disappointment in them may result in rejection of the standards of behaviour which he has modelled on them. This is not to say that he will discard all his loving memories of his parents. On the contrary he may, on the surface, be totally preoccupied with these, while his disappointment and anger express themselves by a relinquishment of some part of his character which is closely modelled on them. It is as if he were saying that for all his love of them he does not want to be like them. If what we say to him about the reasons for his coming into care preserves his belief in his parents' affectionate concern for him, it will not matter so much that they appear weak, and sometimes powerless, in difficult circumstances. An extreme case may make this point: a child who has been deserted by his mother must feel that he is of little value to her. In such circumstances it would be easy for him to reject what she has taught him, and to abandon the model he has constructed for himself with her help. However, it is not impossible to help a child to understand the degree of unhappiness, illness and confusion which led to her taking this step. He certainly will have many memories of her which will make sense to his feelings about what we say. The added understanding which we can give him may enable him to go on loving her and to retain what she taught him. In this event he will continue to be accessible to new relationships and to extend and mature his standards with the help of new models.

We have to admit that many of our children have received inadequate standards from their parents. The nature of their upbringing has been haphazard and misleading and, in some instances, perverse. Even when this has not been so, children subjected to painful separations are not always helped to sustain their good models in the way we have suggested. It follows that any Home is likely to contain a proportion of potentially undisciplined children.

The frustration and hate which the child is experiencing are sometimes so great, and the healing process so slow, more particularly if there have been many such upheavals, that the forces of disruption seize control of his personality. During this period the child's inner structures require active outer supporting agencies. It is here that external discipline is most appropriate to support the ideals and standards which the child has, despite himself, been temporarily moved to abandon.

At such times the grown-up may be inclined to think, when comparing his own children with the disturbed child, that the structures which can be relied upon in the one are totally absent in the other. Yet only in the rarest instances is this true. Such a parent may recall that in periods of great stress his own children will also demand active outer support in living up to their inner ideals. One example of these stresses occurs when the adolescent finds that his structures are threatened not by outer loss but by the newly aroused instinctual forces which make life more difficult for him. Tempted to overthrow his own ideals and standards, he may sometimes even say to his parents, "You don't allow me to do this, do you?", and accept with relief the prohibition he is thus assured of.

With children in residential care the structures we have been describing are often not clearly apparent. The behaviour of such children can often be summed up as beyond control or delinquent, and the effort to help them regain control is not always successful. This condition in a child might, however, never have come about if in the course of his life he had been helped to keep continuity with lost parents or former foster parents and therefore with inner standards and ideals. To be fruitful, any effort at rehabilitation now must help the child to a relationship with a new grown-up. In this relationship discipline and the supporting from outside of his own internal structures will be an important feature. We must not be disappointed if we find that a few of the children with whom we have to deal have so confused and bewildering an internal world that they have become inaccessible to help in the ways which we have at our disposal and that others require such painstaking and prolonged assistance as may tax our patience and ability to the utmost.

It is not our view that any particular child should be allowed to disrupt the community. There are a number of children who can be made to conform to reasonable community standards by applying more than the pressure needed for the average child. Staff are able to tell which children are amenable to such measures and they are usually capable of exerting the extra pressure needed to exact conformity. In these instances children are happier than they would be if their impulses were allowed to get out of control and become excessively disruptive to the Home. In some cases this seems to provide a final solution for the child. It may be that he can by this means learn how to control his rebellious impulses and can obtain reassurance from their successful control. Sometimes, however, such a child may develop other symptoms, such as bed-wetting or symptoms of physical illness.

There is a third group of children who do not respond to the normal affection and discipline of a Home and who are not amenable to extra pressures as are the children we have described in the first group. Nor do they develop symptoms as the second group does. Rather, they become more and more undisciplined. The tendency in this situation is for staff to step up their disciplinary measures until such time as they have to admit exhausted defeat. For the two latter groups there emerges ultimately one solution—namely, that adequate psychological treatment should be provided.

Symptoms

It would be neither useful nor expedient to investigate in detail the many delinquent and neurotic symptoms to which children (even those in their own homes) are prone. A few general statements may, however, be helpful. From birth onwards children may experience frustration of need in many varied forms, with which their immaturity makes it difficult for them to cope. The most favourable situation in childhood is found where the child's instinctual demands are met by normally helpful and understanding parents in an environment which fulfils the average expectations of human beings. We know that these conditons arise more rarely than we should like. Some children seem exceptionally vulnerable at one or other period of their development. Some seem to be greedier in infancy, others seem to be intractably difficult to train in cleanliness and all, perhaps, are prone to excessive jealousy of brothers and sisters, though even here there are considerable individual differences. Some children are helped in these problems by astonishing intuitive skill in their mothers: others are less fortunate. Further, a child's development may be marred by traumatic events in his own or in his parents' lives during his early years. Early separations, parental illness or the child's own grave illness are not infrequent disturbances. It may even happen that three factors; constitutional predispositions, traumatic events and a failure of parental care may come together to make the worst combination for a particular child. A greedy infant, reluctantly fed by a clumsy mother and suffering a digestive disturbance of some severity, meets frustration at his most vulnerable point. One of these conditions operating at a time could perhaps be safely adapted to by the immature organism: the combination of all three simultaneously may well leave a scar. To take another example, a child who is reluctant to be trained in cleanliness may have added difficulties when a new pregnancy, and the mother's anxiety over the management of two babies, leads her to carry through this process faster than the child is willing to go with her. These examples, in which a child's constitution, his stage of development and the environmental circumstances are at variance could be multiplied. Circumstances which would make no problem at one stage would make a real problem for the child if they impinge on a vulnerable point in his development. A mother's illness and removal to hospital in the early years may be a calamity for the child, while in later years he may be mature enough to understand and support this. Unfortunate confluences such as these leave mental scars and weak spots in the child's development. These may not be evident immediately, or the immediate difficulties may be overcome and forgotten. Only when, at some time in the future, the child is subjected to what he experiences as undue stress, will the vulnerable

D

areas disclose themselves again. The child who has been deeply disturbed in the early years by the loss of the mother in the circumstances we have described may experience going to school not as an exciting event in growing up, but as a calamity because it inflames the old scar. A child who has experienced cleanliness training as an unexpected and forcible demand upon him may be distressed by future demands for punctuality and order in areas quite remote from potting problems.

We must therefore be prepared for the fact that children will meet the experience of being uprooted from their homes when they are received into care, the facing of a number of strangers, and the implicit demand that they adjust to a new and unexpected order of living, with very different degrees of preparedness for this situation. Traumatic as it may be for all, some will be structured to meet it without a serious setback in their development. Others, on the contrary, may react with anxiety, which belongs as much to the earlier events which have scarred their development as to the dissatisfactions which arise from their present circumstances. Factors which play a part in the child's ability to face these circumstances without experiencing a disrupting inner crisis, are his age, the degree of independence which he has already gained and the degree to which this is vulnerable on account of earlier scarring. In the more vulnerable child past experience will combine with the present to bring about a protest which is not appropriate to the present circumstances but which might well have been appropriate at the time of the scarring. The child whose point of breakdown was in the stage of cleanliness training may react to the demand to adapt to a new ordering of his life by wetting or soiling—a reaction which was appropriate in the old circumstances both as a demand for attention and as a protest, but which is no longer appropriate and is now unintelligible to the people looking after him. A child whose breakdown point was even earlier may react with a feeding disturbance.

Symptoms are therefore an indication on the child's part that he cannot cope with the pressures he is meeting; that he is incapable of communicating his difficulties and that he despairs of his ability to adapt to the new circumstances or to change them effectively.

Some symptoms are transient, and disappear either when the pressures are relieved and the circumstances change or when the child has found understanding of his situation and support from an adult. Such an adult would be able to talk to the child about his anxieties and support him in looking forward to a hopeful resolution of them. In other children symptoms can be intractable and they will then need skilled treatment.

It is natural for the child care worker to hope to prevent or cure symptoms by the two means at his disposal; namely, the employment of insightful and protective staff on the one hand, and, on the other, the selection of an environment suited to the particular child. Some workers have experimented in different types of placement, in the hope that symptoms which prove intractable in one environment may disappear in another. Others have experimented in types of handling and have drawn conclusions about those procedures which seem to them most effective in removing symptoms. Observation of children in various settings may lead us to conclude that certain symptoms are less prevalent in one setting than in another. For example, feeding problems, which can be outstandingly severe in a foster home, may resolve themselves when the child is transferred to residential care. The more detached handling of mealtimes, which is probably characteristic of most residential staff, is the crucial factor which enables the child to give up using mealtimes to focus attention on himself. Residential staff may have less personal investment in the provision and preparation of meals. They will know, from training or experience, that some children make bids for attention through the rejection of food. In leaving the child free to choose or reject food the staff make it plain that they do not regard the rejection of the food as a rejection of them personally. So the child comes to feel that meals are his own pleasure and satisfaction and is free to take them. In this area psychological knowledge can be simply embodied in a procedure which works for the most part to clear up the superficial disturbance (except in extremely disturbed children suffering from anorexia nervosa). Few observations relating the preservation of a symptom to the particular kind of placement or handling can be so simply or easily explained. Such observations are provocative of thought, but may lead to superficial and specious generalisations.

For instance, a trend has been observed that pilfering of food and money is more prevalent in foster homes than in residential care. It is difficult to say how far this is due to the fact that much more is held in common in a Home than in a private family and that, for a number of reasons, the emotional significance of both food and money may be less apparent in a Home than in a foster home. We suggest, however, that the issue is too complex to be explained so simply: such an explanation by-passes the multiple internal factors which contribute to this symptom. Conversely, some observers would say that enuresis is prevalent amongst children in residential care and tends to clear up in a foster home. Two explanations are offered here. First, that enuresis may be a bid for more personal attention and that the symptom clears up because the foster home offers this in greater measure. Secondly, that a child in a foster home has a wider choice of symptoms which are likely to be effective in registering protest at his deprivation (such as the rejection of food), whereas in the children's Home many symptoms are less effective in the face of the detached and professional attitude of the staff.

All these generalisations are based on the attempt to establish a link between the child's present deprivation and the existence of symptoms. One must comment that children in their own homes also present a variety of symptoms, some transient and some intractable, and that the incidence of these is not positively known and is probably under-estimated. It would be wise not to place the whole responsibility for symptom-formation on the fact that children in care are deprived of life with their own families for longer or shorter periods. While this must be a factor, early scarring, perhaps prior to placement, must not be overlooked as forming a predisposing foundation for symptom formation. This scarring is something which has happened once for all and cannot be affected by types of placement. Our belief in the effectiveness of environmental change in removing symptoms must be qualified by this knowledge.

These observations on trends underline the fact that there is a general recognition now that a symptom is a manifestation of a child's profound dissatisfaction and conflict. It is also clearly recognised now that a symptom signifies that a child is at the end of his own resources in adjusting to the demands made on him and that the onus lies on us to come to his aid.

The problem for the child care worker is not the simple one of clearing up a symptom, as it sometimes seems to be. Symptoms can replace each other as the psychic apparatus searches for the one which will be most effective in the circumstances. At present we have no reliable survey of how one symptom replaces another when a child is moved to a different environment. An even greater problem presents itself here: it is sometimes possible to clear up all overt, recognisable symptoms in a child by one means or another and the result may appear totally satisfactory. Experience shows that such a result is frequently obtained at the cost of character changes, such as pronounced obstinacy, social withdrawal, rebelliousness or undue submissiveness. With this wider view of the situation perhaps we should ask why we are so preoccupied with symptoms. The significance of a symptom tends to vary in proportion to the extent to which it causes practical inconvenience and disturbance, both to the child and to the staff. Wetting and soiling are outstanding in this respect. Certain other symptoms, such as pilfering, are socially maladoptive and, if intractable, must be of great significance for the child's future. In fact it cannot be overlooked that a child's attempt to express himself through symptoms indicates an arrested development and an inability to use fully more mature ways of solving his life problems. They may be a sign of a more general inability to use his capacities later to organise his life in conformity with his intellectual abilities and social potentiality and, as such, need to be taken seriously.

There might, however, be a mitigating element to our grave concern in these matters. With his wide and deep understanding of the difficulties for human nature in adjusting itself to its many bewildering vicissitudes, D. W. Winnicott once said, "I have a feeling that every human being has the right to one symptom." Faced with the intricate problems of child care it is not irrelevant to think that sometimes the elimination of a symptom by inexpert people may give rise to character attitudes producing at least as many difficulties, and sometimes more difficulties, than a manifest symptom does. In case this is felt as a counsel of despair, the writers record their belief in the future of child guidance services as potentially of immense importance in assisting child care workers in the elimation of symptoms. The clinic staff have in their hands a body of knowledge which enables them to approach the primitive scarring processes which influence the symptomatic reactions of children, in such a way as to avoid the formation of gross character distortions.

Child guidance service

It is common experience that when a new child guidance service is set up the staff of Homes look to it at first for very considerable help in dealing with disturbed children. In some cases this help proves efficient, but it is unhappily true that in a greater number of cases staff complain that the disciplinary problems of the Home are considerably added to when children are taken into treatment. When this situation is prolonged in respect of a particular child, it is sometimes because the treatment facilities are inadequate. We do not think that treatment once a week is adequate for the very severe problems which the antisocial child presents, even in his own home, and the problem is exacerbated when such a child is reacting as well to the deprivation of being removed from his own family. Such children require intensive treatment ranging from three to five sessions weekly. It frequently happens that once-weekly treatment brings these children's anxieties to the surface and cannot then offer adequate support to resolve them.

In these circumstances we are all of us apt to blame the child himself for presenting us with an insoluble problem; to blame the present service for its administrative inability to help us; to blame the children's officer for shelving the problem on to the child guidance clinic, and, in some cases, to declare psychology bankrupt because we have no evidence of its hepfulness. We would like to reframe the problem in a way which, while not making it immediately soluble, offers us as a profession a constructive line of activity. Psychology is not, at present, able to solve the problem of all children's disturbances, but it has available to it, knowledge and techniques which *could* deal with the vast majority of children presenting the features which we have described. This is not being done at present because to provide the necessary intensive treatment considerable additional specialist staff would be required.

To talk in concrete terms: in a child-guidance service known to us there is one psychiatrist, one psychotherapist, three psychologists and three psychiatric social workers. If the staff were to be made adequate to the needs of the children's Homes in the area, at least five additional child psychotherapists would be needed, at an additional cost of £8,000 a year. The training of such staff it as costly as a medical training and is usually superimposed on the training of a psychologist or on other types of child care training, for which a university degree is necessary. It is impossible to compute the saving which adequate treatment services could afford to the community. It would certainly be far in excess of the expenditure on salaries. It is to the provision of an adequate therapeutic service that, as a profession, we should direct our efforts.

The development of self-direction within the children's Home

In the children's Home the building of ideals constantly goes on. Certain of the standards are similar to those in an ordinary family, but certain of them are different because the quality of living in a group is different from that in a private household. The demands of conscience can be more limited in many children's Homes because the choice of behaviour is restricted. "Being good" is to some extent related to observing rules of order and routine, which have to be imposed because the space and equipment and the attention of the grown-ups have to be shared out amongst so many. For example, the schoolgirl may be prevented from exercising free choice as to when she will put on a clean blouse, because blouses must all be changed on the same day, whether they are clean or dirty. The boy does not develop a conscience about giving extra work to the housemother by putting mud on the carpet, because outdoor shoes have to be removed on entering the Home, whether they are clean or dirty. These are simple examples, but the restriction of choice and the consequent limitations on the child's opportunities to extend his standards are often still more fundamental.

The inner structures thus built tend to be related to unquestioning obedience and conformity to routine: certain domestic rituals are substituted for the choices of conscience. This thought might sometimes give us pause. It is a healthy thing if, from time to time, we are willing to consider where, and in what ways, our routines form an essential part of community life and whether in some respects we have allowed them to become unnecessarily rigid.

Discussions about discipline are apt to be disappointing to residential staff. Suggestions as to the appropriate procedures and attitudes in such a diversity of human problems inevitably throw upon them more responsibility for painful thinking and decision making. Above all, the decision has to be made in each particular Home as to how far a warden can afford to add to the burden the staff is already carrying for the sake of a few exceptionally difficult children. Protecting the staff from undue strain is an important function of the administrator. It is not possible to make every child into a normal citizen and, if this seems a disappointing conclusion, it must be remembered that there is no magic way of transforming human personalities.

CHAPTER NINE

GROWING UP AND LEAVING HOME

THE SPECIAL FEATURES of adolescence are important enough to justify a brief comment. This does not imply that a different set of principles applies to the care of the adolescent, nor that adolescence is to be regarded as a species of disorder. There is just as much cause for concern over the young person who shows no marked change in mood, interests and behaviour when he reaches puberty as there is over the one whose life becomes exceptionally turbulent at this time.

Many of the books about adolescence were written when social conditions were less flexible and offered young people less opportunity to manifest themselves as fully as they can today. Current studies, on the other hand, tend to stress the social problem presented by young people who have not been able to function well in these more flexible conditions. It should, however, be helpful to those who are concerned with children in care to be clear that a large proportion of the adolescent population living in their own homes is neither withdrawn and depressed nor distracted and abnormally unintegrated. Nor, on the other hand, are they simply younger versions of adulthood.

It is a mistake to imagine that the young person can easily become part of the adult community or that he wants to do so. If he is healthy, he wants to move in a community of young people like himself. For the most part, this community is self-contained. Each young person, however, likes to move freely between the family, where he still largely has the status of a child; the group, where his adolescent interests are accepted by, and discussed with others like himself; and the adult community, where he may have a responsible, if minor, rôle. He does not choose any of these groups to make a permanent status for himself. Perhaps because his sense of himself is so unstable, he needs all three backgrounds to help find himself. We are sometimes impressed by the sense of responsibility which an adolescent can show; sometimes by his ingenuousness and instability and, yet again, by the clinging uncertainty which binds some young people so firmly to their families. All three aspects may succeed each other so rapidly as to make him appear volatile and moody. This amounts to saying that we need to provide him with three environments—a place in the world where he has some responsibility; a group which shares his youthful uncertainty, and a home which protects him from his childish anxieties, while at the same time expecting him to take some share of responsibility within it. To provide this is quite a problem for a normal family where there are rarely more than two or three young people between the ages of fourteen and eighteen to be considered at any one time.

The difficult adolescent

Residential communities provide so many contrasts to this simple situation that it is just not possible to speak about adolescent residential care as if we were dealing with an extension of the family. Even when we consider a single adolescent in a Home where he is the only teenager, we are often dealing with a relatively unstable young person with an unstable family background. Such a young person may well have had a period of some instability preceding adolescence. His unsettled early years may have failed to give him abiding interests and standards in which we can have some trust. This immaturity may make him more demanding of freedom and privileges than the average. Public care normally lasts only till eighteen and our period of influence will therefore be relatively short, though recent legislation permits us to give guidance after that age at the request of the young person. In these cases we must therefore always be uncertain whether we shall be able to lead such young people to a relatively normal adjustment. These considerations give the writers little confidence in their capacity to formulate principles on the upbringing of adolescents in residential care.

A further difficulty derives from the practice of providing for the more difficult adolescents in residential care in approved schools, in hostels for working boys and girls and in children's Homes.

A young person should be sent to an approved school on the assumption that he is emotionally stable, but has been subjected to perverse environmental influences. We expect him to be able to form relationships in the new environment as he has done in the old, but with better consequences.

Hostels for young people over compulsory school age have a wide variety of uses. They are needed for engineering apprentices, for grammar, technical and university students, and in the city for country youths needing accommodation near their work. Again these hostels adequately serve the needs of young people with structured characters.

Children who reach adolescence in the children's Home in which they have been brought up and to which they have made satisfactory adjustment may find that it continues to cater adequately for their needs up to school-leaving age.

But the unstable adolescent is, from his very nature, unable to profit by group life in Homes, hostels or approved schools. He needs, above all, the opportunity to test his capacity to make an individual relationship in a family setting without competition from others of the same age and sex. This may involve him in a series of placements during which he is learning and growing. Whatever measure of adjustment he attains will be the result both of the time given him to grow up and his capacity to assimilate and profit from these changing relationships. In these vicissitudes he must be assured also of stable and understanding supervision from a child care officer. Even so, we shall sometimes be disappointed with the results of such prolonged and painstaking efforts and shall have to admit that our resources are inadequate to prevent a small proportion from becoming recidivists, prostitutes or chronic psychiatric patients.

In attempting to distinguish those adolescents who can profit from residential care, it may seem that we have defined the limits of this group too strictly. It would not be difficult, for example, to cite situations in which disturbed boys seem to be profiting from just such care. For example, in a particular Home for fourteen boys between eleven and fifteen with a man and wife in charge and an active régime, the majority of boys appear to conform readily to the expectations of the staff. They take part in all the organised activities: the team games; the Saturday walks; the Sunday church; the handicrafts; the routine housework; the regular attendance at youth organisations. If they go on a journey it is with the church choir; if they go to a dance it is with the youth club; if they go away for a night it is to the Scout week-end camp. The boys make no disturbing demands for personal freedoms, which would be unacceptable to the staff. If they show any inclination to modify the régime it is wrapped up in a way calculated to make it acceptable. They are not without outside interests, but these are such as would be approved by the Home authorities. There is a general tendency to mass conformity.

There is evidence that boys in groups like this will subordinate to the régime of the Home their normal adolescent wishes for inordinate freedom and their wish for opportunities to make excursions into bizarre experiment. A typical comment is, "Mr. X. would not stand for that." Amongst the boys themselves is a secret understanding about a world of inclination whose coming must be postponed. Occasionally, the staff get a glimpse of this, for example, when they discover notes and drawings with a sexual connotation passing amongst the boys or when they accidentally overhear the conversation in the dormitories.

This is little different from what goes on in a great number of the less articulate private families. We might well say that this outcome is nothing more than the impact of one common kind of parental character upon the kind of child who tends towards being inarticulate or inaccessible to the adult. On the other hand, it is often clear that the relationship between these particular adults and these children might be very different if the organisation of the Home allowed it. In a large group the staff cannot allow a dozen boys the latitude and support which they might allow to their own sons.

Perhaps we should be glad that a situation of enforced conformity gives time for the process of growth. Nevertheless, an opportunity has been lost by using this expedient. The outstanding relationship with the adults in this Home is an artificial one: it offers no support in the child's approach to his immediate problems whilst he is in the Home. Nor does it offer any retrospective support after he escapes from the Home into supposed freedom and in the disappointment which must follow.

Leaving home

It is at the point when any child who has been in residential care starts work that we have to face the fact that the Home makes no pretensions to serve the continuing function of the family. Some of those who leave us as working boys and girls do not regularly return to visit the Home and to share their successes and anxieties with the people to whom they have for so long looked for parental support. They change their jobs and their lodgings, become engaged, married and have children, without apparently feeling that these events are of concern to those who brought them up.

Many children do return at first and get pleasure and satisfaction from their visits, but experience shows that the frequency of their visits falls off after a comparatively short time.

A boy of eighteen was noticed one day by a schoolmaster, sitting on his bicycle leaning against the wall opposite the front door of a children's Home. The teacher knew that George had been brought up in the Home and had left it at fifteen. George asked about his mates in the Home, and the teacher was able to give him news of some of them. But it soon became clear that there were only one or two children still living in the Home who had been there in George's time. And of course these few children had been little ones when George left. The old matron had retired and a new young couple had taken charge in the last year. The teacher thought that there were one or two junior staff, whom George had known, still working there but he could not tell George their names. He told the boy that Mr. and Mrs. Roberts, the new warden and matron, were very kind people, who would be sure to welcome him. But George had not come here to get a welcome, however kind, from strangers. After a few more minutes' talk he shook hands with the schoolmaster and pedalled away.

George clearly experienced the Home leaving him. Whether or not the old matron had retired, the Home which contained many new children was a new place. How do we estimate George's loss in being cut off, in youth, from some sort of continuity with his early up-bringing?

The young person returning to his own parental home will also experience disappointment from time to time. The degree and quality of communication over intimate concerns, whether they be economic ones or the more disturbing aspects of personal relationships; whether they concern jobs or friendships or are specifically sexual, will perhaps increasingly fail to come up to his expectations. He will have ultimately to face the larger gap which exists between one generation and the next, in its most painful aspect. This discovery is clearly a prolonged process which begins in schooldays but finishes in adulthood with the final recognition that responsibility for one's life and its most critical decisions can only rest with oneself. This is a basic truth, in spite of the continued real assistance which the family affords to its younger independent members. Perhaps the chief difference between the homeless child and the child with a family is that the former achieves his separateness in so short a span of time. The possibility of growing in the process to accept that he has absorbed all that the home has to offer, and that he has outgrown it, is rarely reached.

The process of growing up always has frightening features. On the one hand the young person looks forward to a freedom which he can only learn to exercise constructively later by plunging in now. He cannot foresee the problems until he arrives at them in practice—either the problems of the outside world or of his own reactions to facing them. This can only be worked out when he faces an employer and other employees; when he deals with potential sexual partners; and when he is testing himself and is accepted or not accepted in work and in love-making.

The quality of his assurance and hopefulness or of his anxiety and self-distrust must depend on how his home life up to this point has coloured his inner world with one or the other emotion. Whether the child returns to the Home or not, his memories of having been helped and understood within it must affect his ability to tolerate and work through the new anxieties inherent in adult life. He will protect and care for himself in an understanding fashion and have some potentiality for understanding, and even protecting, others. He will be sustained in his difficulties by the belief that it is possible to find and use help in the new environment as in the old. If he leaves the Home with a sense that his wishes and anxieties, from childhood to adolescence, have been in some small measure understood, he will leave with a sense of loss. These memories and these emotions may direct him to look in the right places for what help he needs in the future, and to distinguish real understanding and healthy support from seductive offers of help and spurious reinforcements to his self-esteem. In this, he will be gratefully acknowledging the value of his early upbringing as a springboard to the larger life. Like George, he may at least want to come back.

If he has left in a mood of disillusionment and frustration his approach to the difficulties of adult life will be marked by all the variety of façades which substitute for real satisfaction in rebellious and unhappy young people, rather than with a steady increase of understanding and power.

Difficult adolescent girls

Whereas difficult adolescent boys can, with care and skill, generally be maintained in a state of conformity in a group, this can rarely if ever be done with difficult girls who are not assured of the continuing interest of their parents. One such girl may be all that a Home can contain; two may be four times as difficult. The results of trying to care for groups of deprived adolescent girls under one roof are not impressive. No one is more aware of the intense strain and tension of these establishments than the Heads of girls' approved schools. Their colleagues, the headmasters of the boys' schools, are acutely conscious of the anxiety and withdrawal of the headmistresses, and the staff of the girls' schools are at times subject to anxiety and bewilderment. The people in charge of such communities cannot be held responsible for the outcome. They may be people who could produce different results in a different setting, as their own sons and daughters often demonstrate.

There appears to be an acute biological and psychological problem for girls like this who are forced into an exclusively feminine community. We do not, of course, advocate mixing groups of disturbed adolescent boys and girls, but only that the mode of care selected for a girl should take account of these problems. What mode of care can then be found? Two possibilities offer themselves: first, fostering in a private family (which falls outside the scope of this book) and, secondly, care in a very small children's Home in which there must not be at any one time more than one disturbed adolescent girl. Such a girl may rapidly take her place as the confidante of the matron and her helper, though often an irritating and inefficient one. While she may come to the Home with a reputation for being "an affectionless character who is unable to make relationships", she seems all too ready to show a devouring affection and to demand it in return. In these circumstances, however, this affection can be channelled in a number of different directions.

The younger children readily offer themselves to be taken care of and the staff will see that they are not hurt thereby. The small community, and the girl's exclusive position in it, make it not too difficult for her interest in clothes and cosmetics, with all the adolescent idiosyncrasies which these involve, to be accepted and tolerated and to become a focus for a real relationship with the adults. In a group of adolescent girls, these matters often become a gang concern from which the adult is excluded. The girls make each other more bizarre and more rebellious, thus tending to undermine the status of the Home in the neighbourhood. One older girl on her own in a children's Home may use cosmetics inartistically and excessively and wear ridiculous clothes, and this can be met by critical but tolerant comment. If dirty duffle-coats and tight jeans are accepted without question on Saturdays, the girl may be more ready to conform to a different mode on Sundays. If her preoccupation with personal appearance is encouraged and praised, and her need for privacy is recognised, she may become more responsive to advice about managing her money, particularly if freedom to spend it foolishly is recognised as a necessary prelude to wise management. She will have a bedroom of her own, or one she shares with another, younger, girl. The undertaking of specific household tasks should confer immunity from being called on at any time to do any odd job. In this way she feels valued and esteemed.

Life in the Home will not be easy: there may be quarrelling and defiance, furtiveness and bad language. The girl may run away several times and be welcomed back with less drama than would result in a community of adolescent girls.

At the worst she may get into trouble; but this is not the end of things. It has happened before, and girls have worked through their difficulties to become happy and useful workers, wives and mothers.

Who carries the responsibility?

Some of the stress and anxiety, which leads to breakdown of relationships between girls and staff and which can even lead to a disastrous breakdown for the staff member herself, is due to confusion about responsibility for a girl's misbehaviour. For too long committee members have congratulated the staff of Homes on the good manners of the children, the tidiness of the Home and the absence of delinquency and sexual promiscuousness. If this is the pattern of child care which is considered meritorious, it is inevitable that the thoughtful matron is going to foresee when a girl is likely to get into serious trouble and to inform the authorities that she can no longer take responsibility for her. But the matron should not be led to think that the committee will judge her solely by the good behaviour of her children.

The accolade must in future be accorded to the matrons who soldier on in the face of almost insuperable difficulties, knowing that the reputation of their Home may at any moment be marred by an act of violence or immorality. The responsibility must clearly rest with the authorities who place or leave the child in the Home, not with the skilled and devoted staff who endure the daily peril and exasperation of having such a girl in their midst. The clear acceptance of responsibility by the committee can only be made real to the matron by affording opportunities for her to meet them and to keep them informed of such a girl's progress or lack of it.

The ordinary adolescent

While we have been at pains to make clear that children in care generally present during their adolescence very special problems which can only be managed by a well-informed administrative policy, we cannot leave this topic without taking note of some features of normal adolescence which are relevant to the less-disturbed young people in care.

In Chapter Six, entitled "Separateness and Belonging" we discuss the child's need to have a private life of his own, whilst keeping at the same time a secure base from which he can venture forth and to which he can confidently return. The perplexities which are created for the staff by the co-existence of these two complementary needs are intensified when the child grows to adolescence. We know of the reticence of the primary school child about many aspects of his life outside his home, particularly about school and what goes on in school. This is a major first step in making for himself a private life on a grand scale. In adolescence we must expect an intensification of this attitude and we have to accept it as the child's normal right.

This and indeed every aspect of his adolescent development will owe much to the care he has received in his earlier years and the feelings and attitudes which have resulted from his experience of life in the family. The special feature of adolescence is the maturation of sexual powers, and the special preoccupation of this age must be the drive towards adult sexual and social life and towards getting and keeping a congenial job leading to economic independence.

The young person's attitudes towards sexual freedom and towards the spending of money are inevitably problem areas in his relationship to adults at this time, and family discussions centre largely around these two topics. These discussions can be conducted in a relatively acceptable way or they may give rise to serious tensions. In a family where trouble has been taken to see that communication between parent and child has been established, and maintained throughout the child's life, we will expect to find a better basis for communication at this time. The principles of upbringing which we have expressed in this book are directed to the cementing of sincere interchange between the generations. When this has been established the passage to adolescence may well have been eased. Financial and sexual matters are, however, fraught with tension, more especially perhaps between members of a family, and more especially at this time. Real communication and fruitful discussion about them are not things which can be commenced when a child reaches puberty: they should begin with the confident answering of children's questions in the years of infancy. A mother who is able to recognise when young children's questions are prompted by concern about procreation and about the physical differences between the sexes, already takes her child into partnership in these vital matters. At this time the girl's curiosity is prompted by her desire to establish her femininity, to identify with her mother in numberless feminine ways, and to be loved as a little girl by her father. Sexual instruction at this time is important because it relates so closely to the girl's feelings about herself and the people she loves most. Affection between the parents offers the child a pattern. The confidential relationship with the parent which sexual instruction opens up will illuminate her approach to all the biological events in the family—child birth and baby care and finally her own menstruation. The increases in her emotional and in her biological understanding go side by side. Such a child is in the confidence of her parents from early years, and can make the passage to adolescence without shock and without undue reticence. The little boy's desire to establish his masculinity in identity with his father, and to be loved for this by his mother and, too, his ability to integrate the emotional life of the family with his own masculine rôle can be helped in just the same way. The bridge to puberty is thus built in the earliest years.

The married couple in charge of a children's Home have equal opportunities with a child's real parents to form his attitudes to love, marriage, child birth and even death in this way.

Sydney, aged twelve, from a Home went to spend a few days' holiday with his older brother's widowed foster mother. On the journey back to the Home he was full of anecdotes about her making him feel one of the family. Outstanding in his mind was that she had taken him with her to tend her husband's grave and the graves of her parents. The child care officer was in no doubt that Sydney had learnt something about loyal and tender affection.

Most of the quarrels between the generations in adolescence about the spending of money and time outside the Home are rooted in the fact that freedom to use both are adult attributes. The child resents interference with this freedom because in many ways it is an interference with his sexual freedom. It involves his rights to pass his time with boys and girls of his own age, discussing their common concerns in which sexuality is ever present. It also involves his right to spend money on his own adornment and to establish his rôle with his equals.

John, aged fourteen, frequently received ten-shilling and pound notes in his letters from his father. He did not show the contents of his letters to the staff nor tell them when he received money. The children's officer debated whether to forbid John's father to send more than a moderate sum. But John's father was likely to find some other way of smuggling the money to him and, in any case, it seemed necessary that there should be tangible recognition of the father's need to make up to his son for not being able to look after him at home and of the boy's need, for the time being, to receive these tangible proofs of the father's deep concern. The couple in charge of this small Home therefore decided to put up with the inconvenience of having a boy in their group who disposed of unusually large sums of pocket money and to cope day by day with the obvious problems which followed, such as jealousy from the other children and the risk of outbreaks of pilfering. If they had taken a more rigid line and insisted on opening the letters and taking charge of the money, they would have had a more manageable short-term situation, but John's inner life would have been further pushed into inaccessibility.

The same extravagance which marks the sexual preoccupations of young people also marks their spending of time and money. In this it is hard for the adult to go along with them as fully as they would wish, partly because we fear that they will develop false attitudes and partly because money and time are very real problems for the adult too. Let us also admit that adolescent irresponsibility is a paramount challenge to us. We cannot help jealously contrasting their youth, their opportunities and their freedom from responsibility with our own heavy adult burdens.

It is a wise parent, foster parent or houseparent who can find his way in so complex a relationship and do justice to the children in his care.

CHAPTER TEN

THE CHARACTER AND PERSONALITY OF HOMES STAFF

Helpful attributes in Houseparents

THE MOST IMPORTANT single factor in the building up of family life is the quality of affection and understanding which the parents feel for each other and for the children and the way in which they interpret their responsibility as parents. In the same way, life in Homes also bears the stamp of the personal qualities of the adults in charge.

Those Homes are fortunate where the people in charge are able to give the children true affection and inspire it in return, and where, while accepting their responsibility to modify children's crude behaviour and make them responsive to satisfactory ideals, the staff realise that real and lasting responsiveness to high standards is a matter of slow growth. Such adults are clear in their own minds that they can enlist the help of the children in their own education by other considerations than the fear of punishment alone; they are not misled by the façade of good behaviour, which the inwardly rebellious child can put up to avoid revealing himself, and they go at least half-way to meet the child by ensuring that the standards of the Home are not too far above what is expected of others more fortunate in their own families.

It is easier to illustrate, from fortunate situations, the kinds of personalities that have responded successfully to the demands of caring for groups of children than to attempt to set out the special factors which make for a successful warden. It may be that successful appointments sometimes result from an almost fortuitous harmony of personalities and conditions, and more frequently they may result from a flexible relationship between residential and administrative staff, based on an honest and co-operative appraisal of each other. What the qualities are which make a man or woman acceptable to children in these special circumstances, we do not know. The following descriptions are an attempt to give composite portraits of the kind of people who are giving good residential care to children.

Mr. and Mrs. Roberts run a Home for fourteen boys, nearly all of whom have been committed to care for offences against the law. They have a boy of their own, who has his meals with the others and takes part in all their leisure activities. But they make no pretence at treating him "the same as the others". They say, "After all, the others have parents or relatives or special people of their own." Mrs. Roberts is a quiet, unassuming person, who clearly loves her husband and son and gets immense satisfaction out of running her household. She takes a keen professional interest in the personality and affairs of each boy. Whilst she is fair to all she is inhibited about her feelings and admits it takes her a long time to get to know and to like new boys. She makes shrewd comments about them, and it is obvious that she is not trying to bid for their affection. Nevertheless, many boys return on holiday or write to the Home expressing warm appreciation of the care they have received. Mr. Roberts is the sort of man that youths admire: he is full of simple fun and was a fine footballer in his young days. He takes part in all the activities with boy-like enjoyment, but he is no perfectionist. He is just as pleased when a duffer makes a brave attempt at boxing or batting or making a model boat as he is when he gets a boy into the school first eleven. His boys have caused a lot of trouble in the local schools, but the teachers invariably praise the readiness with which Mr. Roberts co-operates with them on terms of equality, although he is quick to put in a word for any one of his boys whom he thinks is being unfairly treated. Unlike Mrs. Roberts, who is a home bird, he has lots of friends in the town. He knows everyone and they all know him. He plays billiards at the club some afternoons and is not ashamed to spend an occasional half-hour in the public gallery at the police court or watching a mechanical excavator. He often finds jobs and lodgings for boys leaving school, but he is pleased to hand over responsibility to the child care officer as soon as the boys are placed. One thing which endears him to us all is that he takes a pride in sending in brief and often humorous reports on any events of importance to individual boys, particularly about visits from parents. For our part, we know that it is fatal to make arrangements which will interfere with the day and a half each week which he devotes to his private life with his own family. He is a fine example of an unlearned but responsible and happy man. Mr. and Mrs. Roberts seem to provide just the setting in which some boys can have a rest from specially conflicted environments and a base from which they can, with the help of child care officers and teachers and child guidance clinics, begin to renew their relationships with the world outside the Home. Mr. and Mrs. Roberts provide an active régime, with only limited freedom to make a choice. If this kind of boy is given complete freedom to choose for himself he becomes distracted;

he "goes haywire". If he is given no freedom he retaliates with aggression, or bides his time with an outward semblance of obedience without forming any relationship with the adult looking after him: he is "completely untouched" by the régime in the Home. So he is given limited freedom; for example, he is able to choose whether to join the Scouts or the Boys' Brigade, whether he will play cricket on Saturday or go swimming. The adults are interested in what he will choose, and will discuss with him the factors which he will want to take into account in making his choice. The limitation of this kind of régime is that it may produce a rather brittle conformity. This, after all, may well be the best that can be done for boys who have had such disruptive early experiences.

Of course, it is an enormous help if the person in charge of the Home is happily married. The appointment may be a joint one, or the husband may go out to other work. Marriage provides exceptional opportunities for interdependency and the sharing of troubles and responsibilities. But married couples are not alone in making a successful contribution to this kind of work.

Mrs. Holmes is a widow with one daughter. She runs a Home for eight boys and girls in a poor part of the town. The standards of clothing and supervision of the children are not exceptionally high and the children are always scuffing round the streets in their spare time like the other children in the neighbourhood. A visiting observer said, "Of all the Homes I've seen, this one is the most integrated into the community in which it is set." Like her neighbours, Mrs. Holmes rather keeps herself to herself, and she looks down on those who gossip on the pavement. She derives immense pleasure from organising her household, and her assistants have to fall in with her ways or leave. But the last assistant stayed for five years and only left to get married. Mrs. Holmes has warm relationships with her late husband's family. She arranges for her daughter to go and stay with them for a good part of each holiday so that she shall experience life in an ordinary household. She is a great rank-and-file worker in the social life of the parish church, a devotee of the local repertory company and a soroptimist, though she would not think of accepting office in any organisation. She encourages parents to visit, though she can be strict with those who turn up in a drunken or obstreperous mood. She seems to be able to enter into the children's feelings about their own parents and to give them unspoken sympathy. As a child she had an ordinary elementary education, but she has a quick intelligence which, in these days, would probably have taken her to a grammar school. She has immense confidence, born of long experience of successful upbringing of children. She does not expect the children to be something different from what they actually are. Her own sense of security is based upon the love and admiration which she inspires not only in the children but in the committee and the child care officers and upon the fact that she has a clearly defined rôle. She gets anxious if it is suggested that she should extend her functions beyond the confines to which she is used. Like a good mother she will go to the school when there is an open day or a medical inspection and she is pleased when the children bring home better school reports, but she really has little interest in the children's schooling. ("I leave that to the teachers, that's what they're there for".) This happy capacity to shut herself out of those parts of the children's lives which are not her direct responsibility is also shown in her relationships with the child care officers. When other people impinge directly upon the happiness of a child in the Home she can be forceful. This makes her indignant with parents who fail to keep their promises to write or to send parcels or to visit. But her anger derives from her sympathy for the child: it is quite different from the aggressiveness of Miss Green, referred to later, who viewed the parent as a rival for the child's affection.

Even when the spouse is dead, the fact of having experienced marriage, and of having had children, will generally mean enlarged horizons and will have given more confidence in the capacity to make relationships. But marriage is not a *sine qua non* for the head of a children's Home.

Miss Moore is in the fifties. She came into residential work in early middle age, having been put out to service at fifteen and having subsequently been a nannie in a succession of private families. She adopts a professional attitude to her work and probably welcomes the approach of retirement on pension in the same way as she looks forward to her annual leave and days off, which are spent with friends and relatives. She has no theories about child care, but very definite ideas about right and wrong. Interviews and correspondence with children whom she has brought up show that these ideas have made a great impression upon many of them. Miss Moore does not compete with the parents for the children's affection, and some observers would say she is rather cool in her attitude to the children. She never minds a child going home or to a foster home, so long as the reports say that the household is satisfactory: indeed, she often presses for the less disturbed children to be boarded out before they get too used to the way of life in a Home. She feels that life is hard and that both grown-ups and children had better face it pretty grimly and undemonstratively. The keynote of Miss Moore's rather formal and unexciting upbringing of children is her absolute rectitude and dependability. The children learn that within her clearly defined rôle she is firm as the rock of Gibraltar. Her greatest contribution has been in caring for the long-stay child who has extremely unreliable parents. The child's devotion to a phantasy parent is fully acknowledged and Miss Moore is able to say clearly to the child that she understands how he must be feeling: she sympathises with his hope that things will become different, whilst helping him to see that it may take a very long time for things to change. Miss Moore fulfils that part of the parent's duty towards this child which is not forthcoming from the real parent, without striving to supplant the parent's place in the child's affection. She is the first to accept the limits of her own capacity, and she occasionally asks for the removal of an exceptionally difficult child on the ground that the child is beyond her understanding and needs skilled care from persons with psychiatric knowledge, and in this her judgment is probably sound. One would not choose Miss Moore for the upbringing of a total orphan who had no clear memories of his own parents: but there are so few of these in residential care that this is not, in practice, a limitation of Miss Moore's usefulness.

A good matron of the old P.A.C. days was *Miss Wilkins*, who retired soon after the Children Act, after thirty years in charge of a cottage Home. She had very limited intelligence and breadth of vision, but she was quiet, unstimulating, undemanding and reliable. The children swam forward at their own pace in a quiet and sluggish stream. Many children found years of security with Miss Wilkins and grew up to lead uneventful lives. They often came back to see her, bringing their wives and children, but when they had drunk a cup of tea and passed the time of day there was little left to say, and no conversations beginning, 'Do you remember the time . . .?' Many had experienced with Miss Wilkins a placid and contented childhood with few demands made on either side. One wonders what this did to the more enterprising and intelligent.

Miss Lang was miscast for the long-term care of children, but found her métier as matron of a short-stay Home. She was an intelligent and much travelled woman of good education. She sparred with the children like a kindly professional pugilist teaching boxing to a particularly unpromising bunch of youngsters from the D stream of a primary school. She was detached from the children, but not withdrawn from the world. She had a stimulating life outside the Home and stuck as rigidly as possible to her scheduled days off and holidays. Her attitude was, "I do this competently for a living, but I have a life of my own apart from the children".

The man's part in Home life

The last four examples show how a woman on her own can make an important contribution to child care as Head of a children's Home. The idea of appointing a married couple has sometimes been advanced in too facile a manner, like a dependable recipe, whereas those with experience of making these appointments know that one of the major difficulties is that husband and wife are rarely equally well suited to the job. It often appears that one husband from amongst a number of couples is eminently suitable, whereas the best woman for matron is partnered with a less suitable man. Whereat the committee wag proceeds to propose that husband number one and wife number two should be appointed. The full-time man in charge of a modern, relatively small Home has to be an exceptional kind of fellow. He will generally be happiest if he is by nature a handyman and gardener who can potter about the place whilst the children are at school. He may be a virile man who likes to devote a lot of leisure in the daytime to manly pursuits, like golf and fishing, so that he becomes a shift-worker who is employed in the evenings and early mornings and week-ends and who puts in a hard day's play from Monday to Friday. He needs to have the satisfaction of a solid day's activity, in addition to the exacting but somewhat sedentary responsibility of being Head of a Home. To be good with children you need to know how to enjoy your own leisure as well as take part in theirs.

The advantages of having a man as well as a woman in charge of a Home are too obvious to need emphasising. With the arrival of the forecast excess of men over women in the population it seems likely there will be far fewer single women and widows available for employment in the future and that married women, whether or not employed jointly with their husbands, will play a bigger part in residential child care. No doubt they will come to be appointed to posts which are at present the almost exclusive preserves of single women, such as the appointments of Heads of Nurseries and of girls' Remand

Homes, Hostels and Approved Schools. Meanwhile, the value of having a man about the place in these four types of establishments is not to be gainsaid. In the area best known to us there are one or two highly successful Nurseries with married matrons and one mixed Remand Home (staffed by four married couples) which has coped with many a girl who has previously proved a severe trial to an exclusively feminine establishment.

If the matron is unmarried, special care should be exercised in the selection of subordinate male staff: the gardener at a residential Nursery should be chosen at least as much for his attitude to rearing children as for his experience of raising vegetables. Such a man has one advantage not shared by the full-time superintendent: he has specific daily work to do which is recognised as such by the children, so that they get into perspective the father's part as a person with a job which regularly takes him away from exclusive preoccupation with the family, and that he has a right and a duty to be preoccupied with matters outside the household. The separate, distinct, functions of the two parents in an ordinary family are thus emphasised.

Problematic personal traits

It is the most natural thing in the world that those who make the decision to give up their whole time to living with children should want the children to love them. But a number of children in Homes are unable for the time being to show affection for anyone; and many more have their warm feelings directed towards their real parents or to phantasy parents whom they contrast unfavourably with the people who are looking after them.

Everyone in residential work has to come to terms with these difficulties in different ways and sometimes a particular way of coping may create its own new problem. Sometimes the residential worker makes a virtue of necessity and dedicates herself to a life of undue sacrifice, which is harmful in its repercussions on the children and prevents the worker from presenting to the children an example of a properly self-protective personality. One feature of such Homes is that the children who seem to be best integrated in their relationships with such self-sacrificing staff can tend to grow up to be unable to share interests and relationships in wider circles.

There is a marked contrast between the Home which is run by people with a normal love of their work and an interest in surrounding themselves with contented people, and the Home which is a setting for some forceful and unbalanced drive or ambition, in which the staff have to satisfy themselves first of all, and at whatever cost to the work and to the children. Such qualities are not always discernible at first sight and are seldom without compensating attributes which derive directly from them.

Here is a fictitious description of the kind of Home which was sometimes encountered in early times. We will call the matron "Miss Green". Any resemblance to any living person is coincidental.

Miss Green ran a small Home for eight children, which was the pride of the neighbourhood. The children from the Home were always entered as a team for everything that was going: the carnival procession; the children's dramatic competition; the relay race in the bank holiday sports, The children were beautifully dressed—all alike, like a prep. school. Matron delighted to take the children on every kind of outing, sitting amongst them on the front seat of the bus and entering heartily into all their interests. The Home was open house to other children from the neighbourhood and it was whispered that some of these children had expressed the wish to go and live in the Home.

Miss Green had an intense personal interest in the children; she made them feel they were wanted, and went to no end of trouble to see that they had plenty of interest and activity. Children who seemed forlorn and deprived in the larger Homes were moved to Miss Green's, where they quickly began to look lively, stopped bed-wetting for the time being, and developed an easy camaraderie with grown-ups.

Parents were, however, reluctant to visit their children in the Home, and were relieved when, exceptionally, they were moved to another. When Miss Green was asked if the children had heard from their parents the answer was almost invariably, "no", although a talk with the children about the contents of their lockers would reveal carefully treasured letters and Christmas cards from home. One rather dull boy of nine was found in possession of a substantial toy, which had been sent by his auntie: but he did not seem to know who had sent it and set little value upon it.

Miss Green always reported that the children were "good as gold", but fairly frequently someone ran away.

In this kind of régime, would it be possible for children to be loved for their own sakes or would they be implements to serve the matron's love of power and popularity? Good assistants would not stay; except for those who were detached from the situation, having their main interests outside the Home, and doing the job for the sake of board, lodging and wages.

The extent to which divergent qualities in staff neutralise each other and ultimately limit the progress of which the children are capable, is shown in the following example of another matron, who carried self-sacrifice too far.

[1] At first sight, this home appears to have everything against it. The children are wild, noisy and untidy, and seem to have no respect for adults, or consideration for each other. The Home is grubby, especially the bathrooms, and seems to be rapidly breaking to pieces. On further contact, however, we modified our opinion.

We gather that almost all the children have been completely cured of their enuresis, and they have the frankness and self-assurance one usually associates with the "public school" type of child. Their manners too, if this is taken to mean their social easiness and contact with adults, are charming. But we think that this result is being obtained at too great a cost to the endurance of the matron and that it shows mis-guided self-sacrifice on her part.

We therefore doubt whether she will be competent to continue the experiment to the point of building up the necessary positive self-discipline in the children. In spite of her desire to establish a community, we do not feel that there is as yet any community spirit. The children obviously have complete confidence in her and feel wanted and safe. She reveals genuine affection for them and concern for their well-being, rather than for her own comfort, but does not understand where her self-sacrifice should end and the children's social education begin. We think she could be helped by training.

Some wardens have educational theories of their own which, though apparently enlightened, are hazy and grounded in sentiment rather than real knowledge and experience.

This hostel is run by a group of progressive people who are well-educated and have an interest in child study, but who lack adequate training. There is a general dabbling in psychology without any sound knowledge. Influenced by the single concept of freedom, the staff have taken no steps to discipline the children. Windows are broken, furni-ture and play material is smashed up, there is considerable truanting

[1] This report, and many others in this book, are taken from Ruth Thomas' *Children without Homes* (see Bibliography, No. 27).

and outbursts of uncontrolled behaviour. The staff show great forbearance, indeed far too much, and the hostel will not effect good results by these methods. They are trying out half-fledged theories on the children very unfairly.

Competence in housekeeping is very frequently commented on by workers visiting every type of Home, but in contexts that give point to a statement published by Mr. Leon Willshire, the former superintendent of the P.A.C. Homes and subsequently first children's officer for Southampton, when he said, "In practice, the foster mothers (in Homes) tend to be women who are sound in house management rather than home management." Some matrons prefer to concentrate on housekeeping, especially when the children are proving difficult.

The house is well kept, the feeding good, the clothing seen to and the children well cared for, but Mrs. H. has not much idea of how to manage a child nor of how to love him, though she is kindly enough. It is perhaps her ignorance which makes her possessive and at the same time liable to use repressive measures when children are unresponsive.

The Home is spotlessly neat and clean, shines everywhere and is furnished pleasantly. The only "but" is that no group of children could keep up that standard without constant reminders. Matron is inclined to be on the defensive, and more eager to run her Home well according to her domestic lights than to get to know and understand the children.

The matron says the Home is run on hospital lines with definite time off for all the staff (five for nine children), and one feels very strongly that the place is run primarily for the staff's comfort. The material side of things is excellent, and the children are treated in a kindly way, but there is condescension rather than genuine sympathy in the contact between children and staff. It is not surprising in these circumstances that there has been no improvement in the enuresis or other behaviour problems.

Choosing staff

The features to be looked for in the selection of residential staff are rather different from those which determine most local government appointments. The selection committee will not be especially impressed by education, or qualification, or even by previous experience: many a good Home has been started by people without experience. Far more important is the quality of the family life of the applicants; not only their family life now, but whether they themselves in childhood had a good measure of loving relationships. To assess this requires special skill in interviewing: the applicants who can be brought to talk easily about parents and brothers and sisters with whom they are still in contact will give the committee some idea of the quality of their relationships. If the committee find that any approach to discussion about family experience is embarrassing to the candidate, this is likely to have a significant bearing upon the applicant's capacity to make a secure home for children.

We conclude in the hope of having made it clear that the key to the residential care of children lies in the appointment of staff who have training and insight into children's inner needs and who are themselves happy people, kept happy by skilled and considerate administration.

Part Two

VARIETIES OF RESIDENTIAL CARE

CHAPTER ELEVEN

INTRODUCTION

Mᴜᴄʜ ᴄᴀɴ ʙᴇ done for the child in care by the resident staff in their internal management of the establishment, but their endeavours are dependent upon the existence of administrative machinery which is equally well-informed about the children's needs and which is ready to provide the organisation and the establishments which are necessary to meet those needs.

The function of the administrator is threefold: first to see that there is sufficient variety of residential provision conveniently situated in relation to the area served; secondly, to ensure that the conditions within each establishment are such as will enable the staff to go some way towards meeting the children's needs as they have been discussed in this book; and thirdly, to see that the resident staff are supported by the organisation, in their relations with the wider community, with the parents and families of the children in their care and with the committee and other persons exercising authority. In this Part we describe various kinds of residential care which are provided for children in England and Wales at the present time.

The needs of a particular authority or voluntary organisation for residential establishments will depend in part upon the nature of their population and terrain, in part upon the philosophy and ideas about child care which are held by those who formulate the policy and direct the management of the agency, and in part upon the particular need which the agency has been set up to meet.

Anyone who attempts a survey of the different kinds of residential care for children will be struck at once by the fragmentation which has resulted from the piecemeal development of the child care services. A need has been observed, and sooner or later establishments have been set up to meet the need. Subsequently, attempts have been made, with varying degrees of energy and success, to integrate the separate establishments into the broader system of child care services. Strength as well as weakness derives from having a wide span of child-caring agencies: for example, the co-existence of children's Homes run by charitable societies and those administered by public authorities has left scope for experiment as well as for choice on the part of parents in the selection of modes of care for their children. Weakness is apparent in the rigid segregation of the approved school child and the mal-adjusted child from the main stream of child care.

A map of the residential child care services therefore has ill-defined boundaries, and no two draughtsmen would produce exactly the same document. The criterion for the inclusion of any type of establishment in the following description has been that at least some of that type seek for the time being to make up to the children in some degree for the loss of home life. Home life may be lacking for some purely temporary reason, such as the absence of the mother from home due to a short illness or confinement; or it may be permanently lacking due to a child's being orphaned, or totally abandoned by parents whose whereabouts are unknown. It may exist over a long period without amounting to severe deprivation, for example when the parents' vocation takes them to live for years in a distant part of the world from which they nevertheless remain constantly in communication with, and responsible for, their children. It may amount to severe deprivation even though the parents are immediately and constantly accessible; for example, when a father commits a sexual offence against a daughter, in consequence of which the girl and her sisters may be prevented by a court order from visiting their own home, although they may be constantly passing the house and seeing their mother daily. We have excluded from the list such establishments as hospitals and boarding schools whose rôle is not to provide a substitute for family life.

In formulating the descriptions of types of residential establishments, and particularly in assessing each type, the writers have been influenced by the philosophy of upbringing, which is described in earlier chapters, and their experience in particular areas of child care.

Residential establishments can be grouped into three main types:

I. Those providing primarily for newly admitted children.
II. Those providing long-term care for children without exceptional needs.
III. Those providing care for children with exceptional needs.

These main groups may be subdivided according to structure and purpose.

In applying this threefold classification to *small Homes* and to

Nurseries it becomes apparent that establishments of these two types do not constitute homogeneous groups. Some small Homes are intended for the long-stay care of relatively stable children and are generally staffed by a married couple, the husband following his own occupation. These are called "family group Homes". Other small Homes are used mainly for children whose behaviour is disturbed, and these have to be more heavily staffed, so that the grown-ups can have regular holidays and time off. The children do not stay here to grow up, but only so long as they need to be helped to adjust to life: they then go on to their own homes or to foster homes. We have entitled this type "Adjustment Homes". Similarly, some agencies use their Nurseries almost exclusively for newly admitted children: after the child and his social setting have been investigated he goes back home or into a foster home. We call these "Reception Nurseries". Other Nurseries are used mainly for children for whom foster homes cannot be found and these children are often suffering from various kinds of disability and may be considered to need special nursing care. This is the traditional type of Nursery which keeps most of its children to the age of five or later. We call these simply "Residential Nurseries" and classify them amongst those establishments which provide for children with exceptional needs. There is no systematic national census and classification of most of the establishments we attempt to describe. Exceptions are Approved Schools and Remand Homes, concerning which precise statistics are published by the Home Office. For the rest we have examined such figures as are available and have estimated numbers, size and cost to the best of our ability, where possible taking into account establishments belonging to voluntary societies, which cater for about a quarter of all the children in care. When we have consulted published material as a guide to our descriptions and estimates the sources have been indicated at the end of each section by a reference to Part II of the Bibliography. All the estimates relate to England and Wales, in which there was in 1963 a resident population of 47 million persons of whom 13 million were children under eighteen.

Where it has been possible to estimate the average cost of maintaining one child for one week this has been stated at the end of the section as a "unit cost". Many of the estimates are based upon the joint publication of the Institute of Municipal Treasurers and the Society of County Treasurers, entitled *Children's Services Statistics* (Number 23 in Part II of the Bibliography). Unit costs can, however, be misleading because they vary widely according to the extent to which the available accommodation is actually occupied. A Home for ten children, having only five children in residence throughout the year, will show double the unit cost which it would have shown if it were fully occupied. Furthermore, the unit costs of recently built Homes include an element for loan charges (mortgage repayments of capital cost), whereas an older building will have been fully paid for.

CHAPTER TWELVE

ESTABLISHMENTS FOR NEWLY ADMITTED CHILDREN

THE RECEIVING HOME

Description and Purpose

RECEIVING HOMES ARE owned and maintained by local authorities and voluntary societies. Such a Home may be a house on its own or one of a group of cottages in an estate of children's Homes. It provides immediate shelter for children on admission, often in emergency, and caters for the more obvious needs, such as medical examination, of new arrivals; cleansing and outfitting; rudimentary observation of the child, and assessment of his likely future needs. It acts like a lock gate in protecting the level calm of the long-stay children's Homes from an uncontrolled, turbulent ingress of new children.

History

Receiving Homes were established by some agencies in the late nineteenth century and the first half of the twentieth century in response to an obvious need, though many agencies did without them and admitted children direct to long-stay Homes. Since 1948 many have been closed and superseded (especially in the local authority service) by the more refined Reception Homes, which are described later.

Number of children, age and sex

Size can vary greatly, according to the needs of the agency. A unit as small as eight beds may be attached to a larger building. A large agency may have a unit of fifty beds. Usually the children are of both sexes, and of school age only, a child over or under the limits of compulsory school age being admitted only in exceptional circumstances.

Staff

A married couple or a single woman, without special qualifications, will be in charge. Assistant housemothers will bring the ratio of total child care staff to children up to about one to every four or five children. The irregular hours and extra laundry and cleaning demand a strong domestic staff.

Special features

In many respects the features of a Receiving Home are similar to those which are attributed to Reception Homes further on. The Reception Home is rapidly superseding the Receiving Home, but the latter may still have a part to play, especially in those agencies where the needs of the child may have been largely discovered at leisure in his own home before reception into care. Receiving Homes differ from Reception Homes in that the children are almost always sent out to the ordinary day schools. They generally lack special facilities for the psychiatric and psychological assessment of children, relying upon the ordinary child-guidance and Hospital Board services should these be required for a particular child.

Number of establishments, location and cost

The number of Receiving Homes is not known, but they have diminished in number since 1948. The majority of them were placed fairly centrally in relation to the population which they served. It was common for Receiving Homes to be conveniently close to towns, since the location of many was fixed before the advent of the motor-car. Estimated unit cost £10 in 1964.

Refs. See bibliography: *16*, paras. 166, 178, 232, 482-4; *24*, p. 30.

THE RECEPTION HOME

Purpose

Sub-s. 15(2) of the Children Act, 1948, says that any local authority's residential accommodation must include separate provision for the temporary reception of children with, in particular, the necessary facilities for observation of their physical and mental condition.

The Reception Home makes a reserve of accommodation available to meet any ordinary eventuality: it cushions the long-stay Homes against sudden admissions and violent fluctuations in demand. It provides an opportunity for the child and his family to see their problems in perspective. The child is for the time being removed from some of the more immediate family stresses. If he has come away from home in an acute emergency he is given skilled help in coming to terms with and understanding the reasons for his removal. Where this is done under a judicial order the same applies but, in addition, the family are given expert help in reassessing their attitudes in the light of the judicial action. Future plans can be founded upon leisured observation of the child and his family.

It should not, however, be supposed that the majority of children need to be admitted to a Reception Home on first coming into care. In the first place, many children come into the care of local authorities for short periods, and the occasion does not warrant assessment of their needs in a Reception Home. Secondly, even those who are expected to remain in care for a long period may have their needs assessed before they come into care and can then go straight to foster homes without the additional disruption of moving into, and out of, a Reception Home. In some authorities as many as eighty per cent of children admitted for long stays go straight into foster homes.

An important feature of the work of the Reception Home is the reassessment of need of the child already in care who has had for some reason to leave his foster home and for whom fresh plans have to be made.

The Reception Home may be used as an Observation Home and as a Remand Home for children under fifteen. These two functions will be described later. It may also be used as a short-stay Home for children in temporary need of care, for whom foster homes cannot be found.

Description

Reception Homes are owned and maintained by local authorities and by a few large voluntary societies. Some are purposely built, but most of them are large, old dwelling-houses which have been specially adapted.

History

The establishment of Reception Homes was one of the major recommendations of the Care of Children Committee ("The Curtis Committee") which reported in 1946. A pilot experimental Reception Centre was set up under voluntary auspices with the co-operation of the Kent County Council in October, 1947. An interim report relating to the first year's work was published in 1948 and the experience gained provided the basis for a Memorandum of Guidance issued to local authorities by the Home Office in April, 1951. In the ensuing thirteen years a good number of Reception Homes have been established by the larger local authorities, and many of the smaller authorities have made arrangements to share the facilities of each other's Reception Homes. Knowledge and experience in relation to Reception Homes are accumulating over the years. There is still much to be learned and there are still wide divergencies in the use of Reception Homes and in the conduct of such Homes.

Number of children, age and sex

Maximum accommodation will vary according to the population served, and will generally be between fifteen and forty. It nearly always caters for both sexes. If the agency has the use of a separate Reception Nursery it will not normally be necessary to admit children under five. Even so, very young children will usually be admitted if they accompany older brothers and sisters. The upper age limit is normally eighteen, but consideration is given to the likely effect on each other of containing several older difficult boys and girls at the same time. In circumstances where the presence together in the Reception Home of older boys and girls would be disturbing, the Remand Home can provide alternative segregated care.

Staff

Usually a married couple is in charge; but exceptionally a single woman. Some training in social work or in the care of children is expected, and if a couple offer experience in teaching and nursing this is especially acceptable. Another married couple or a single woman assist the people in charge and deputise in their absence.

Assistant housemothers, in a ratio of about one to every four children (varying according to age), working on shifts, attend to the daily care of the children. Nursery nurses and Nursery assistants, in the ratio of one to two-and-a-half children, are employed if there are several children under about four years old. A higher ratio is needed when babies are cared for.

A specially strong domestic staff caters for the wide variety of need, the irregular hours and the extra laundry and cleaning consequent on the frequent admission and discharge of children.

Special features

(i) The newly admitted child is likely to be frightened and resentful, whatever face he may put upon his troubles. He needs an immediate approach by skilled staff informed as to the reasons for his coming and trained to give him the understanding and assurance which are necessary in his circumstances.

The child may have been removed from home compulsorily by judicial action; his parents may have deserted him and disappeared, or may have been taken, protesting, under his eyes to a mental hospital or a prison; they may have suffered a maiming or fatal accident in his presence. No one may be able to tell him what are the chances of his going back home, or of even seeing his parents again. When the circumstances are simpler, as when the mother has gone to hospital for a minor operation or a confinement, the child, especially the younger child, still feels a measure of rejection, carrying within it the unconscious idea that he is somehow responsible for his apparent banishment and that he is no longer loved and valued by his parents. Where the home has been a turbulent, neglectful and unhappy one, his fears are likely to be accentuated, not relieved, by the orderly life and material comforts of the reception Home. The contrast makes him feel all the more strange, and the superior standards of the Home constitute an unspoken condemnation of his parents. He may feel that the staff, in their very helpfulness, are competing against the parents to provide a better home and capture his affection.

Staff with the high qualities of sensitivity and perceptiveness needed in these circumstances are not easy to find. If they have these qualities, they may be peculiarly vulnerable in the special circumstances of the Reception Home. Their satisfaction has to be found in using their professional skill to help a succession of children, rather than in building lasting relationships with a more permanent group. It is by emphasising how the plan for the child's future rests on the contact and understanding which they can supply at this juncture that the staff are enabled, year after year, to work effectively and with satisfaction.

(ii) In this situation of stress, provision for the children's medical and psychiatric care and for their schooling must be given special thought. It is helpful if, when he is newly admitted, the child can go to school on the premises. He should not be faced with the necessity to relate to curious and insensitive schoolmates in still another new setting. Individual attention in the small schoolroom in the Home enables a quicker and closer assessment to be made of his personal and educational difficulties. But the following groups of children may go out to the ordinary schools:

Those who are sent to the Home because of truanting or school phobia.
Those who are within reach of the schools which they normally attend.
Those needing grammar and technical schooling.

Those who have been in the Home for some weeks and are likely to remain still longer.

It will be helpful if there is a variety of schools within reach of the Home.

(iii) The moment when a child comes into residential care may be a time when a number of new influences are brought to bear upon his family, with far-reaching results. The opportunity may be present to mobilise casework resources in a way that will help the family to a sounder footing. The rôle of the child-care officer is crucial here. It will be helpful to her if the distance between the Reception Home, the child's own family and other agencies whose assistance she needs is not too great. She will also be helped if the Reception Home is situated within the authority's own boundaries, so that she is using her own police, education, health and children's services and not those of another authority. This makes for a quicker resolution of problems by administrative action.

(iv) In the early days of Reception Homes special attention was directed to the length of a child's stay in the Home. The authorities were anxious that children should not stay indefinitely and that they should not become attached to the staff and then suffer a further disruption in their relationships. Sub.s. 15(4) of the Children Act, empowered Parliament to make Statutory Regulations limiting the duration of a child's stay in a Reception Home, but after a few years' experience it was made known that these powers would not be used: it would be left to the discretion of local authorities to decide how long each child should stay. The majority of children leave Reception Homes within three months of their admission, but it is impossible to be more precise than this because the children's circumstances are so varied. It is not unusual for a child to leave after a few hours' stay occasioned by some temporary crisis at home. On the other hand, in very exceptional circumstances, a child's stay may be prolonged for as long as a year, during which a series of situations in the child's own family are being resolved under the guidance of the caseworker.

Number of establishments, location and cost

There are a little under 100 Reception Homes in England and Wales. They are placed, so far as possible, conveniently to the populations which they serve, and are generally in or close to a town so as to take advantage of urban amenities and services. Unit costs in 1962/63 varied between £8 and £23; average £12.

Refs. See bibliography: *4; 12; 16,* paras. 482-3.

THE OBSERVATION HOME

Description and purpose

The name "Observation Home" was used by a Government Committee on Maladjusted Children in 1955 to describe an establishment which would provide for the observation, in a residential setting, of children thought to be in need of psychiatric treatment. Such a place might be called a "residential, diagnostic child guidance clinic". There are few, if any, Observation Homes in existence in Britain. Children not in care of children's committees needing residential observation are at present admitted to psychiatric hospitals or to publicly or privately maintained hostels for maladjusted children. The Government Committee (in a document popularly called "The Underwood Report") recognised that separate Observation Centres were unlikely to be set up soon, and they recommended that Reception Homes run by children's committees should have the scope of their service widened to serve the additional function of receiving and observing children who would not otherwise be in care.

History

Since 1959 local health authorities have been empowered to place and maintain mentally disordered children in Homes provided by children's committees, under the provisions of S. 9 of the Mental Health Act, 1959. This enables Reception Homes to be used as Observation Homes, but the power has, as yet, not been used much, and there is little experience of its usefulness. It may be that the psychiatric services in their present state of development do not find a widespread need for such facilities, or that many children's committees are not in a position to offer the service at present because of other, more pressing, demands.

Number of children, age and sex

These would be the same as for Reception Homes. Older children whose behaviour was too disturbed for care in an Observation Home would be cared for in a psychiatric hospital.

An Observation Home would have staff similar to that of a Reception Home. There would be specially close links with the staff of a child guidance or psychiatric clinic, and the Home might be run under the direction of a psychiatrist or a psychologist rather than of a social worker.

Special features

These are similar to the special features of Reception Homes. An important difference from the Reception Home is that the child in an Observation Home is there voluntarily, by the wish or consent of his parents and possibly with his own tacit consent. In this he differs from the child in care, who is in the Home either because his parents cannot for the time being provide for him or because he is away from home by Order of a Court. The different circumstances need to be fully understood by the staff of the Home, so that they can discuss the situation as it develops with the child and his family.

Number of establishments, location and cost

As far as is known, no separate Observation Homes have yet been established. There are a little under 100 Reception Homes in England and Wales, and these are potentially available to receive children for observation. They are spread over the country in locations convenient to the population served and to urban amenities. Estimated unit cost £12 in 1962/63.

Ref. See bibliography: 6, paras. 245-6.

THE RECEPTION NURSERY

Purpose

The Reception Nursery aims to look after children under five who have to be received in emergency. It may also be used instead of a hospital for observing and diagnosing a child's medical condition. Its purpose is similar to that of the Reception Home. The growing trend against the use of residential care, especially for younger children, has resulted in many long-stay Nurseries gradually becoming Reception Nurseries without being formally recognised as such.

Description

Reception Nurseries are owned and maintained by some local authorities and some voluntary societies. A few are purposely built, but many are adapted from large old dwelling-houses. The cost of adaptation is high and the results are generally disappointing and inconvenient. Rapid changes in demand and changes in ideas about the best types of planning have brought about a confused picture of Nursery care in Britain at the present time.

At one time horizontal segregation was practised: a baby graduated from the baby unit into a "tweenie" unit and then later into a "toddler" unit. More recently, Nurseries have been organised into "family groups" of between four and six children each, under the care of a nurse and an assistant nurse. Accommodation has been adapted and rearranged to ensure that the "family" is able to sleep together and have their meals together and to be looked after continuously by one or other of the two family nurses. In a few Nurseries very young babies have been introduced into the family groups. Since, however, a child under six months is unlikely to be in residential care unless he is thought to suffer from some medical condition, it is generally felt wiser to have a separate unit for these delicate babies.

The most recent tendency is to build a central block to house the matron and senior and specialist staff, together with a medical room and a unit for up to six babies, and to build other houses in the same curtilage, each to house a family group of about six children aged one to five with two or three staff. The establishment may have its own nursery school or some of the children may go out to school.

History

Residential Nurseries have a very long history. In the nineteenth and early twentieth centuries it was customary for Poor Law Authorities to house their younger children in one or more wards of the General Mixed Workhouse, which was later renamed the Poor Law Institution. Whilst older children were taken out of the workhouse and placed in District Boarding Schools or in Grouped or Scattered Cottage Homes, the youngest ones remained behind under the general supervision of the workhouse matron, being looked after by unskilled staff, who were often assisted by inmates of the workhouse. In the 1930's there was a general move away from the workhouse into separate, autonomous, establishments. This move was hastened by the War of 1939-45, when many children were evacuated to the country, and some workhouse wards were damaged by bombing and some were taken over for other uses. The social upsets of war and the increase of illegitimate births made increasing demands on Nursery beds, and health committees of local authorities exercised their powers to set up Nurseries independently.

When the Children Act of 1948 set up children's committees, it imposed on them the duty (by Sub-s. 13(2)) to close the last remaining Nurseries in former workhouses. Large numbers of new Nurseries were opened, based on the models evolved by the Poor Law and Public Health Authorities. Within a few years the development of boarding-out programmes (placement in foster homes), especially for younger children, resulted in many areas in a diminution in demand for places in Nurseries. Where these programmes were successfully implemented it then became necessary to reduce the number of

Nurseries, leaving only enough accommodation to serve the needs of those younger children who could not be placed in foster homes immediately on admission to care. These therefore became Reception Nurseries. In a few areas even the Reception Nurseries have now been closed, their place being taken by foster mothers and by small nursery units in Reception Homes.

Number of children, age and sex

Reception Nurseries vary in size from an ordinary house with four or five children up to a large establishment for fifty. They commonly have between twelve and twenty-four children of both sexes. Most Nurseries cater for all ages prior to starting school—namely, from birth to the age of five. There has been resistance to allowing children to remain on in Nurseries after starting school because of the risk of spreading infection when some Nursery children go out to school. However, if it is likely that a five-year-old will be going to a foster home or returning to his own parents in the foreseeable future, an authority may arrange exceptionally for the child to remain on in the Nursery and to attend a day school.

Staff

In charge will be a matron and a deputy matron, one or both of whom will generally be state registered nurses. Then there will be a nursery teacher or nursery warden, unless the children go out to nursery school; a number of qualified nursery nurses and a number of assistants, who may be sixteen-year-old girls or nursery nurse students. In a Nursery divided into family groups the ratio of nursing staff to children cannot be less than one staff to two children and, even then, allowance must be made for more staff if any of them are students under training. On the domestic side, cooks and cleaners and, generally, a gardener/handyman who (unless some of the nursery staff are married) may be the only man in direct contact with the children, are needed. The total staff for a Reception Nursery of twenty children is unlikely to be less than fifteen and may well be a little more.

Special features

Opinion has been flowing for twelve years or more against the use of residential Nurseries except for Reception purposes. It has been observed that some (though not all) children brought up in Nurseries show emotional disturbance and retarded development later on. A child living in a Nursery, however well it is organised, seems almost bound to suffer, for example, a retardation in speech development.

The deleterious effects of Nurseries may have been exaggerated, but they are marked enough to justify considerable caution in their use, especially for long-term care.

Number of establishments, location and cost

It is impossible to estimate the number of Reception Nurseries, because these (unlike Reception Homes) are not administratively distinguished from long-stay establishments for children of the same age. It is certain, however, that the number of Nurseries being used almost exclusively for reception purposes is increasing and the number of long-stay nurseries is diminishing. Reception Nurseries have perforce to be located conveniently to the populations which they serve. Estimated unit cost £13 in 1962/63.

Refs. See bibliography: *13*; *15*; *22*.

THE REMAND HOME

Purposes

(1) To provide a place where the child can be looked after and detained until he can be brought before a court, and then, if necessary, to provide for him again until the court can, at an adjourned hearing, reach a conclusion as to his future.

(2) To allow for the observation of the child away from his home surroundings. Remand Home superintendents submit reports to courts about the child's condition and behaviour whilst he has been away. Any necessary medical, psychiatric and psychological investigations are conducted whilst the child is in the Remand Home.

(3) To allow for the observation of the child's home and family whilst the child is away. Social workers are able to assess, for example, whether the parents show concern and want to keep in touch with the child and have him back, whether they are relieved and pleased that he has been taken away or whether they have mixed feelings about him. Overtly rejecting parents often display a change of attitude in response to a court hearing and the child's temporary removal as well as the opportunity for discussion with a probation officer.

(4) To provide a place where the child can wait after committal to an Approved School, pending the finding of a vacancy.

(5) To detain the absconder from an Approved School, pending return to the School.

(6) To enable the court to impose up to twenty-eight days' detention in a Remand Home by way of punishment and correction for an offence which could, if the offender were an adult, be punished by

imprisonment. This method of dealing with a young offender may only be used if none of the other methods by which the offender may legally be dealt with is considered suitable by the court. As detention centres become available, courts will no longer have the power to commit to a Remand Home for this purpose.

(7) To provide a secure mode of temporarily looking after the older child who is already in the care of a local authority. This power is contained in Sub-s. 13(6) of the Children Act, 1948, and cannot be used for more than twenty-eight days at a time in relation to a particular child without the prior approval of the Secretary of State. It is used for older boys and girls who cannot be contained in ordinary children's Homes by reason of repeated running away or violent behaviour. This mode of care cannot be continued indefinitely and, after a child is admitted to a Remand Home under this provision, it is then necessary to plan for his long-term care, possibly by an appearance before a court or by admission to a hospital under the Mental Health Act.

(8) When designated by the Secretary of State under S. 11 of the Children and Young Persons Act 1963, to perform the function of a Classifying Centre for children committed to Approved Schools. Classification is explained below, in the next section of this Chapter.

Description

There are one or two Remand Homes which have been purposely built, but the great majority are in large houses which have been converted for the purpose. A good many are in the country where large houses are more readily available. The régime is adapted to short-term care, since few of the inmates remain for more than three or four weeks. In the boys' Homes, emphasis is laid upon brisk discipline and upon the type of activity which can readily be picked up and dropped again. It is important that there should be adequate, trained staff to give individual attention to each boy and to discuss with him the situation in which he finds himself. The girls' Homes receive a minute proportion of all the girls in the community, and these girls are generally very seriously disturbed. There is, therefore, still more emphasis upon individual counselling, and the régime is directed towards inducing calmness of mind by fairly quiet pursuits, such as handicrafts and needlework, rather than upon stimulus to extended activity. Schooling is provided for those who have not reached school-leaving age. A proportion of school children entering Remand Homes are found to be retarded or backward, and special attention is directed to giving some help in overcoming educational difficulties. This kind of help may also be given to young people over school-leaving age. Secure custody is a primary function, and the children are constantly under unobtrusive surveillance. The aim is to retain custody of the child by the personal influence of the staff, and there are few abscondings. It is generally necessary, however, to lock the outer doors of the building at night and to have a supervisor sleeping in a duty room near to the dormitories. In girls' Homes it is necessary to have a detention room where a girl who has shown herself likely to abscond can be prevented from doing so by being locked in. The use of the detention room is strictly controlled. A record of its use must be kept and it must not be used for more than a very limited period for any one girl. In detention rooms means of communication with the staff must be provided.

History

Remand Homes were established in the 1930's by the major Local Education Authorities. The duty was imposed upon them by S. 77 of the Children and Young Persons Act, 1933. Previously, some children on remand had been kept in voluntary Homes and in accommodation provided by members of the Police Force. During the last thirty years a comprehensive system of Remand Homes has been established by local authorities making joint arrangements between themselves for this purpose. Generally, the larger authorities provide Remand Homes, and these also receive children on remand from other authorities. During the War of 1939-45 the need for Remand Homes increased substantially, and many new Homes were opened. The need decreased in the early 1950's and a proportion of the Homes were closed. The special difficulty of planning Remand Home accommodation is that children subject to Approved School Orders, who are awaiting vacancies in Approved Schools, are kept in Remand Homes until there is a place for them in an Approved School. Any increase in the number of approved school committals cannot be provided for by the approved school service for many months, or even years. A large part of the burden of increased committals is therefore thrown upon the Remand Homes. In the early 1960's it was often found that there was not a single place available within reasonable reach of the court to which a child on remand could be sent. It was not unusual for children to be conveyed over 200 miles to the nearest Remand Home having a place available. This was costly in terms of money and also in terms of the time consumed by members of the Police Force in escorting children to and fro, and by probation officers and other social workers in visiting the child in his Remand Home to prepare reports for the court.

Number of children, age and sex

Boys' Remand Homes generally provide for between twelve and forty. There are one or two larger boys' Homes in big cities. Girls' Homes tend to be smaller: between eight and twenty-five. In sparsely populated areas exceptional arrangements may have to be made for girls because there are not enough of them on remand at any one time to justify the expense of a separate establishment. For example, a Remand Wing may be attached to a Reception Home, sharing the staff and some of the facilities of the Home, but affording some degree of segregation from the other children in the Home. The maximum age for committal to a Remand Home is the seventeenth birthday. It is not usual to commit to Remand Homes children under the age of ten, as these are generally more conveniently looked after in Reception Homes. Courts can commit offenders under the age of fifteen to "Special Reception Centres" provided under S. 3 of the Children and Young Persons (Amendment) Act, 1952, in those parts of the country where Reception Homes have been designated as Special Reception Centres.

Nearly all Remand Homes provide exclusively for one sex or the other. A Remand Home specially built before the war for the accommodation of boys and girls in the same building was abandoned some years ago. Nevertheless, there have been, and still are, one or two successful mixed Remand Homes. These are generally staffed by a number of married couples. Special care has to be taken to ensure segregation at night and a high degree of surveillance has to be maintained. The boys and girls generally have meals in the same dining-room and mix for educational and recreational purposes. There is a tendency towards further experimentation of this type, since it has been particularly noticed that girls who become virtually unmanageable in segregated Remand Homes often settle down when they are moved to a mixed Remand Home with some male staff.

Staff

The heads of boys' Remand Homes are usually, though not always, trained teachers. It is common for a man and wife to be jointly appointed as superintendent and matron, and the matron often has nursing qualifications or experience. Girls' Remand Homes nearly always have a single woman in charge, and in some cases she will have teaching, nursing or social work qualifications. The larger Homes have deputy superintendents and deputy matrons in addition. The main body of workers in Remand Homes are called supervisors. Some supervisors have qualifications as instructors in various trades. Boys'

Homes and the larger girls' Homes will have a cook and some domestic staff, but some of the unskilled housework is done by the boys and girls as part of their daily activities. Where teaching is done on the premises, there may be one or more trained teachers in addition to the superintendent.

The staffing of Remand Homes needs to be generous to provide an adequate service at peak periods of demand and to ensure that the boys and girls are kept in safe custody and under surveillance all the time. The smallest girls' Remand Home cannot be run without three resident staff so that, when one is on leave, the other two can still have some time off each day. An adequate staff for a Remand Home for fifteen boys would be superintendent, matron, deputy superintendent, three male supervisors, cook and domestic; and larger Homes would need extra staff in proportion.

Special features

Children found to be in need of care, protection or control (or awaiting appearance at court on those grounds), as well as offenders, may be committed to Remand Homes. However, Sub-s. 51(2) of the Children Act, 1948, requires that non-offenders should, so far as possible, be looked after in Reception Homes rather than in Remand Homes. The legalistic distinction between a young person charged with an offence and one who is beyond parental control or in moral danger is less emphasised now than it used to be, and the better informed courts send children to custody in those establishments which best meet their needs rather than to strive for the segregation of those who have been brought before the court as offenders. In practice it is found, especially in girls' Remand Homes, that a young person charged with stealing may well be more manageable, and less liable to corrupt others in the Home, than one who is in moral danger.

The special difficulty of providing remand accommodation is that the demand fluctuates wildly, and this fluctuation is enhanced by the rigidity of the approved school system. Nearly all the pressure consequent upon an increase in approved school committals has to be borne by the Remand Home service. On the other hand, the total demand for Remand Home places is very small, especially in rural areas. To provide separate boys' and girls' Remand Homes within reasonable reach of the courts in country areas is so costly as to arouse public criticism. Once in the 1950's a girls' Remand Home was occupied for weeks at a time by only one girl, being looked after by three resident staff and a domestic and a gardener. Various solutions have been sought: either by making arrangements with distant authorities for the joint use of Remand Homes (thus entailing long journeys from the court to the Home) or alternatively by making remand facilities available in Reception Centres.

There can be little doubt that the system will be substantially modified in the coming years as the child care service becomes more integrated.

Remand Homes have changed enormously since they were first established thirty years ago. The staff is different; the régime is different and life for a child in one of the better Remand Homes is not necessarily more irksome than in a Reception Home, a Hostel or a Children's Home. Nevertheless, the Remand Home is classified administratively in the same way as its thirty-year-old prototype and is hedged around with rules derived from the Prison Service, which are based on the assumption that the child temporarily detained under a judicial order needs to have his remaining personal liberties defined in a way which is not considered necessary for other children in the residential care of local authorities and voluntary societies. It is more realistic to view all care of children away from their families, for whatever reason, as an interference with common human rights, which is only justified when it is exercised for compelling reasons in a responsible way. If such a view were adopted a selection according to the particular need of a child could be made from the whole gamut of residential provision; Hostels, Homes, Reception Homes, Remand Homes and Residential and Approved Schools. The mode of care provided for a child would not then have to be changed simply because he had been moved from one administrative category to another (for example when a child on remand appeared at court and was committed to the care of the local authority). Furthermore, in sparsely populated areas one well-staffed establishment could serve a variety of purposes: a Hostel could also serve as a Reception Centre and as a Remand Home. The insistence on fragmentation means either that necessary facilities are not provided within reasonable reach or that, if they are provided, they have for reasons of economy to be inadequately staffed and equipped and are not used to the best advantage.

Number of establishments, location and cost

There were, on 1st January, 1963, 32 Remand Homes for boys, 19 for girls and 3 for both sexes, giving a total of about 1,100 places for boys and 340 for girls. As far as possible, they are placed conveniently to the centres of population and are generally shared between a number of Authorities. In sparsely populated and remote parts of the country it is difficult, owing to the small number of children needing remand home care at any one time, to place Remand Homes within reasonable reach of the communities which they serve. Unit cost £14 10s. 4d. in 1962/63.

Refs. See bibliography: *10*, paras. 263-79; *21*.

THE CLASSIFYING APPROVED SCHOOL

Purposes

The general purposes of the approved school system are described below in Chapter 13. The special purposes of Classifying Approved Schools are as follow:

(1) To provide a place where children newly committed to Approved Schools can be gathered together and prepared for admission to long-term training schools.

(2) To facilitate the observation and assessment of the history, characteristics and needs of the child and of his family.

(3) To ensure that the child is allocated to the training school most likely to meet his special needs and to provide for the care of the child until a vacancy arises in that training school.

(4) To provide the training school with detailed information about all relevant aspects of the history and characteristics of the child and of his family.

(5) To provide a centre for research into the causes and treatment of delinquency.

(6) To provide secure accommodation for the custody of children who habitually abscond from the ordinary training schools.

Description

The Classifying Approved Schools are each controlled by a body of managers; lay people who have been appointed *ad hoc*. They derive their authority from the certificate of approval which is granted by the Secretary of State and which can be withdrawn by him if he is dissatisfied with the way in which the School is conducted. Practically all the running expenses of the schools, and the maintenance costs, are met from public funds, but the ownership of the buildings is generally vested in the Managers, who sometimes have at their disposal endowment funds which have been the subject of charitable gifts to the school in former times. The buildings themselves are institutional boarding schools, generally built in the nineteenth century as reformatory schools, although pleasant and convenient modern additions have been made in most places. The régime is like that of an exceptionally large and well-staffed Remand Home.

History

Classifying Schools were set up during the War of 1939-45, when there was an increased demand for places in Approved Schools, in order to make the best use of the facilities available. Since the war they have played a developing role in the approved school service and they received statutory recognition in S. 6 of the Children and Young Persons (Amendment) Act, 1952. They are becoming increasingly recognised as centres for discussion and research into the needs of the approved school service.

Number of children, age and sex

Classifying Schools accommodate about a hundred children each, of all ages likely to be subject to approved school committal orders. This is from about twelve up to the seventeenth birthday but, exceptionally, a boy younger than twelve may be committed. The girls' Classifying School caters for girls between the fourteenth and seventeenth birthday although, exceptionally, a girl already subject to an approved school order may be sent for "re-classification" over the age of seventeen. There are no mixed Classifying Schools.

Staff

The head of a boys' Classifying School is generally a married man whose wife may or may not be employed as matron of the School. The heads of girls' Classifying Schools have always been women. These posts are considered to be key positions in the Approved School Service and the persons appointed are almost invariably graduate teachers of long experience. A Classifying School needs to be exceptionally well staffed with teachers, supervisors and houseparents, as well as with specialists, such as educational psychologists and social workers, who assist in the observation, assessment and reporting. The staff is completed by cooks, domestics, gardeners and handymen.

Special features

(i) A Classifying School is equipped to conduct a more intensive investigation of the child's need than can, at present, be done in any except the largest Remand Home. Since the process of classification is concentrated into a few centres for the whole country, the very best staff is made available and a special body of knowledge about classification is built up. In particular, Classifying Schools have a unique knowledge of the special characteristics of the training schools to which the children will be allocated.

(ii) The régime is adapted to the care of children for short stays only, while they are helped to come to terms with their new situation and to look forward to moving into a training school. It is also able to some extent to absorb variations in the rate of committal to the schools. If there are many vacancies in training schools, the children can be passed on as soon as a decision has been reached: if there is a shortage of vacancies the children can be retained for a little longer without harm.

(iii) In addition to selecting the best training school, the Classifying School is also able to detect those children whose condition is such that they should not be sent for approved school training; for example, psychotic or severely subnormal children, or those suffering from an organic condition such as tuberculosis.

Number of establishments, location and cost

There are four classifying schools for boys and one for girls. A second classifying school for girls was closed in 1960, because of the difficulty of retaining staff. The boys' classifying schools are situated in the north-east, north-west, south-east and south-west. The girls' classifying school is in London. Estimated unit cost £16 in 1962/63.

Refs. See bibliography: 7; 10, paras. 177-83; 19, paras. 233-58; 20, paras. 259-710; 21, para. 5.

THE INTERMEDIATE HOME

Purpose

The establishment of Intermediate Homes was recommended to local authorities by the Home Office in a *Memorandum of Guidance* issued in 1951. It was thought that children coming into Reception Homes would be observed and would have their needs assessed within a few weeks and that many of them would then need to wait somewhere until the right placement could be found—for example, a foster home or a place in a residential school. At that time it was thought that it was harmful to children to wait in Reception Homes after their needs had been assessed, and it was therefore suggested that Intermediate Homes should be set up so that the children could move on there from the Reception Home to wait for a final placement. It was also thought that some children would need a longer period of assessment than could be provided in a Reception Home and that some

Intermediate Homes should be reserved for the accommodation of children whose assessment was in doubt. It was suggested that Intermediate Homes could be combined with short-stay Homes.

In practice, it has been found that there is little need for Intermediate Homes. When the *Memorandum of Guidance* was issued it was not appreciated what a high proportion of children going into Reception Homes would return from there direct to their own families, nor how successful local authorities would be in finding foster homes within a reasonable time. It was also supposed that children would have to wait in Intermediate Homes before they were posted on to residential schools at the beginning of the new school term or the new school year. It is nowadays recognised that a placement in a residential school is only secondary to providing a child with a secure home base, either back with his parents or in a foster home or in a long-stay children's Home.

Number of children, age and sex

Intermediate Homes approximate to Reception Homes and take children of both sexes between the ages of five and sixteen, and also younger children exceptionally. Numbers range between twelve and thirty.

Staff

There might be a married couple or a single woman in charge, and assistant housemothers to bring the staff ratio up to about 1 : 5 (including the people in charge). It would not be usual to employ persons with any special qualifications.

Number of establishments and costs

There are no reliable estimates.

Refs. See bibliography: *12*, paras. 12 and 13; *24*, pp. 50-52.

THE SHORT-STAY HOME

Description and purpose

Short-stay Homes are maintained by some of the larger local authorities to look after children who come into care for short periods (while, for example, their mothers are temporarily in hospital). It is used as an alternative to short-stay boarding out when suitable short-stay foster mothers have not been found. It is more economical than using places in a Reception Home, and it protects the children in long-stay Homes from the disruption of experiencing a continual coming and going of short-stay children. Usually a large dwelling-house is converted for this purpose.

History

A few short-stay Homes were established by Public Assistance Committees before the Children Act, 1948. More such Homes were opened in the decade following 1948, when there was an increase in the number of children coming into care for short periods and the staff of child-care officers had not been built up to operate schemes of boarding out for short periods. With the development of short-stay fostering the need for short-stay Homes is less acute, but they still find a place in some thickly populated areas. A few voluntary societies which cater for children with special handicaps also run short-stay Homes, but the larger voluntary societies have no separate Homes for this purpose: if a child is admitted for a short period he is cared for in a Home which is not exclusively devoted to this purpose.

Number of children, age and sex

The number of children is generally from fifteen to twenty-five, of both sexes. A small authority may not need so many places as this and may have a rather smaller Home. Generally only children of school age (five to fifteen) are provided for, but one of a number of brothers and sisters, who is slightly below or above these limits, may occasionally be admitted to be with the rest of his family.

Staff

It is usual to have a single woman in charge. Occasionally a married couple may be employed, or the matron may be a married woman whose husband goes out to work and helps his wife in the Home in the evenings and at week-ends in return for his board and lodging. There should be a house mother capable of taking charge when the matron is away and one or more assistant house mothers bringing the resident staff ratio up to one for every five children. A non-resident cook and domestics may also be employed.

Few people find the short-stay care of children as rewarding as looking after a more stable group, especially when there is not the added interest of detailed assessment and planning such as is found in a Reception Home. Consequently, the number of suitable people offering themselves for this kind of work is small. Nevertheless, there are those who welcome the opportunity of giving comforting support to a succession of children whose family life is temporarily discontinued.

One such person, Miss Lang, is described in Chapter Ten of this book.

Special features

(i) Experience in child-guidance clinics and elsewhere shows that behaviour disorders and neurotic symptoms often manifest themselves following a troubled period of care away from home. The short-stay Home, which is sometimes regarded as the Cinderella of the residential services, can perform an important therapeutic function. It is often difficult to estimate the length of a child's stay. This uncertainty, and its likely effect on the child, is a factor which has always to be borne in mind.

(ii) Short-stay Homes are particularly liable to experience violent fluctuations in need, being sometimes overcrowded and at other times having a relatively small number of children to look after. Overcrowding is an evil which cannot always be avoided, but so-called "under-occupation" may be welcomed as an opportunity for the staff to become refreshed and to give special attention to the needs of the few children remaining in the Home.

Number of establishments, location and cost

The number of short-stay Homes can only be guessed. Perhaps there are fifty such throughout England and Wales. It is essential that they be placed close to the populations which they serve, to facilitate smooth and rapid admission and discharge and to ensure that the link with home is preserved by relatives and by the child care officer. Estimated unit cost £8 in 1964.

Refs. There is no literature specifically on this topic.

THE MOTHER AND BABY HOME

Description

Mother and Baby Homes are owned and maintained by voluntary societies and by a few local health authorities. They are generally buildings which have been adapted from some other purpose, such as private residences. Nearly all are detached houses with gardens.

Purpose

To provide care and accommodation for the expectant mother who cannot remain in her own home; to ensure adequate medical care before and after the confinement; to provide an environment in which the mother can be counselled and helped to make plans for her own future and that of the baby; and to provide accommodation where she can be enabled and helped to look after her baby until she returns to the community. In some Homes confinement takes place on the premises. Many Homes also provide emergency accommodation for young women who are temporarily homeless and who might otherwise be subjected to moral danger.

History

Mother and Baby Homes were established by voluntary initiative in the second half of the nineteenth century and onwards. Their principal aim, in former times, was to reclaim the mothers from what was supposed to be an exceptionally promiscuous life. The rise in the number of illegitimate births during the Second World War led to increased interest from the Ministry of Health, and local health authorities were given a special responsibility to care for unmarried mothers and their babies. Most local health authorities now either provide Mother and Baby Homes or (more frequently) contribute to the cost of voluntary Homes. The effect of this work is demonstrated by the marked decline in the differential death-rate between the legitimate and the illegitimate infant.

Number and age of girls

Most Homes have between ten and twenty girls, and numbers in excess of twenty are not recommended. Some Homes provide specially for the very young girl, and others are willing to take older women. It is thought best not to have too wide an age range. Most girls coming into these Homes are in their teens and early twenties. Older women are usually able to make some other arrangement with the assistance of the ordinary maternity hospital services.

Staff

Approximately half the Homes in the country have matrons who are state registered nurses and midwives. The other half have matrons with varying or no qualifications. The salaries vary, but are nowhere very high. A few matrons are also required by their societies to undertake casework in the community. In several Homes the only other resident assistance comes from domestic workers and, in a few Homes, the matron is the only person resident. This is undesirable; it means, for example, that expectant mothers going into labour may have to travel alone in the ambulance to the maternity hospital. Some Homes have a qualified nursery nurse or some other responsible woman resident, in addition to the matron.

Special features

(i) The expectant mother needs a quiet routine in which she can gain some security after what has probably been a disturbed adolescence. A recent unpublished survey by the Ministry of Health showed that the Mother and Baby Homes provided this quiet security, but that, on the whole, they did not make the most of opportunities to widen the girls' interests. Mothercraft and relaxation classes, which are particularly important, especially for first pregnancies, were lacking in some Homes. There were fairly wide divergencies in the type of régime, varying from the permissive to the punitive. In some Homes the girls' correspondence was still censored, but this was becoming rare. Only in two Homes did the Matron attempt to prohibit smoking entirely. In most Homes the girls went out in the afternoons in groups of two or three and in some Homes they were allowed out together in the evenings, provided they said where they were going. In all Homes the girls do some domestic work according to their condition: naturally the care of their own babies is put first in every instance.

(ii) At one time it was customary for a girl to be admitted six weeks before the expected date of her confinement and to be discharged six weeks after the baby's birth. The importance of flexibility is now generally recognised. Some girls, because of their home circumstances, need to be admitted for a longer period than six weeks before the birth. After the baby is born, the attitude of the girl's family often changes radically and the family is willing to receive the mother and baby home at once. It is then unnecessary to insist on six weeks' further residence in the Home. On the other hand, many mothers need longer than six weeks in which to make plans for the future. It is not uncommon for mothers to stay in the Home for at least three months after the baby's birth and, in some instances, there are arrangements for the mothers to go out to work from the Home and to return at lunch-time and for the night so that they can attend to their babies. Some agencies find it difficult to provide for the working mother in this way alongside the expectant and nursing mothers. Other agencies, with exceptionally small and well-staffed Homes, are able to make this provision.

(iii) To look at provisions for unmarried mothers and their babies in another country may highlight differences in approach, which on the one hand distinguish one nationality from another and on the other offer constructive features for consideration. For this reason we include here a short description of the Villagio Della Madre E Del Fanciullo in Milan. This private organisation, directed by Signora Elda Scarzella

Mazzocchi, provides an exemplary contribution to the Italian problem of illegitimacy. Originating at the time of the liberation of Northern Italy in 1945 and continuing to the present day, its outstanding feature is the opportunity which it provides for mothers to remain as long as they wish and their needs require. The extent to which Italian village and community life excludes the expectant and unmarried mother and repudiates her condition makes this a peculiarly profitable provision. It supports the expectant mother when she is likely to be confused and despairing, and carries her through for a time, sometimes a lengthy one, until she can establish herself in the community again. In this she is helped by most enlightened social work. This may include an attempt to modify the attitude of her parents when possible, and often, too, the attitude of the putative father. Successful marriages have resulted in a number of cases. No application is refused if the Villagio has a vacancy. Mothers of more than one child may therefore be included in the community of the Villagio. As a result it became necessary to conduct a small nursery in which older children can participate and which serves as a training school for expectant mothers in the handling of children as they grow up. The longer period of residence of course enables young mothers to learn about baby care. The psychiatric social worker attached to the Villagio spends considerable time discussing with mothers the care of children of all ages, and this educational process has shown remarkable results in a country where the systematic study of child care is not widespread.

In Britain it might be felt that such tutelary provision was unnecessary, since we have a more flexible approach to illegitimacy. It may even be felt that other services such as the infant welfare centre already provide what is needed by all mothers. Many people who run Mother and Baby Homes feel that it is detrimental to the child's interests to leave him for a long time in the exceptional atmosphere of the Home. However, the work of the Villagio highlights the opportunity for educational work with mothers and for their social rehabilitation which may still have significance for the services in this country.

Number of establishments, location and cost

There are about 170 Homes, well distributed throughout the country, many dioceses of the Church of England maintaining one or more. Estimated unit cost £7 in 1964. In calculating this cost a mother and her baby are counted as one unit.

Refs. See bibliography: *8*; *26*.

CHAPTER THIRTEEN

ESTABLISHMENTS FOR LONG-TERM CARE

"THE FAMILY GROUP HOME"

Description

THE HOUSE IS generally purposely built or else is adapted from a "council house"[1] or from two such houses.

It contains a living-room and a dining-room which are shared by children and staff; a kitchen and outhouses, a number of bedrooms, and toilet accommodation. Some of the Homes, built to a Home Office specification, also have a small private sitting-room for the staff, a "hobbies" room for the children and a small utility room near the kitchen, for laundry work.

Purpose

"Family group" Homes are intended to simulate family life for children in long-term care. They are used for some children in the care of local authorities and voluntary societies, who do not present severe behavioural difficulties, but who cannot for the time being be placed in foster homes, either because they are brothers and sisters whose interests would not be served by separation from each other into different foster homes, or because of other factors militating against boarding out.

History

A number of Homes of this type were in existence before 1948 and were known as "scattered Homes" because they were generally scattered around a town and its surrounding countryside in order to avoid the difficulties inherent in accumulating numbers of children into a large unit. The old scattered Home differed from its modern successor in that it was rarely built for the purpose: it was usually adapted from a private dwelling-house, and furthermore the persons in charge were generally subordinate to a superintendent and matron who lived in one of the larger Homes and administered all the scattered Homes in the

---

[1] A "council house" is a dwelling erected by a local authority for letting to a private family as part of a scheme of housing improvement: it is generally situated in a group or estate of similar houses.

district. There were a number of centralised services which might include the planning of menus; bulk purchase, storing and distribution of supplies; laundering and repair of clothing and bedding; payment of pocket money to the children and the operation of a system of rewards and punishments designed to maintain discipline among the children. Relief staff moved around from one Home to another to give the person in charge a weekly day off. A child presenting behaviour problems or needing special care could be readily moved from one Home to another, more suitable, without losing touch with his former associates. The system provided for a measure of autonomy for the person in charge of each Home together with advice, support and control for the Superintendent when it was needed. In the early 1950's the idea of having a Superintendent for a group of scattered Homes lost favour: people of a more responsible calibre were appointed to the Homes, which were progressively made more autonomous and answerable directly to the Children's Officer who might be situated in a remote county town. Those persons in charge of Homes who have had experience of both régimes are almost unanimously in favour of autonomy.

Side by side with the conversion of "scattered Homes" to "family Homes" has been a widespread programme of building new Homes. These have been erected in accordance with model plans provided by the Home Office or else have been converted from Council Houses. In the early 1950's, by restricting capital expenditure for the building of any but the smallest Homes, the Home Office ensured that these should have priority. Some large cities built as many as fifty such Homes in the first ten years after 1948. Having appeared to enjoy the special favour of the Curtis Committee, the "family Home" became something of a panacea. It is only in very recent years that experience has shown the particular weaknesses which are set out below under "special features".

Number of children, age and sex

Numbers vary from six up to twelve, but are usually between seven and ten. Most of the children are of school age but, exceptionally, there may be one or two younger or older children. They usually provide for both boys and girls in the same Home.

Staff

The person in charge may be a single woman or (more often) married with her husband going out by day to his ordinary work. There will be some part-time non-resident domestic help and some provision for a "sitter-in" to enable the married couple to have an evening out together.

Special features

The "family Home" has many obvious merits. It would be un-realistic, however, not to point out the following special difficulties, some of which are inherent in the practice of appointing a married woman whose own children and husband live in the Home, the latter following his separate employment:

(i) The husband may not have any special skill with, or interest in, children. If he has, he may have exhausted his tolerance of children during his day's work: for example, if he is a teacher or social worker.

(ii) Appointments to the Home are limited to those married couples who can accept an anomalous situation whereby the family home is provided as remuneration for the woman's work.

(iii) The couple's own children cannot be treated differently from the other children in the Home. There are no rooms private to them and no assistant staff to release the parents and enable them to function from time to time as a separate family entity.

(iv) The real family must always take their holidays with the children in care. Husband and wife can rarely spend evenings outside the Home together. It is not sufficient that the agency may employ a weekly sitter-in.

(v) The duration of a couple's willingness to be employed in this type of Home is unpredictable. There is no certainty that any one set of children will receive continuous care until they are grown up. The demands of the husband's job may enforce a move. The stress inherent in this situation seems to cause an unusually large number of these couples to separate. The situation compels husband and wife to seek their outdoor recreations separately. This offers peculiar temptations to the husband, especially since his desertion would not result in his wife and children being deprived of home and income.

If a family Home can avoid the difficulties cited above it offers some compensations, in keeping brothers and sisters together in a family atmosphere until each in turn leaves to go out to work, and in pro-viding homely care for children for whom a foster home has not been found. The "family group Home" should be sharply distinguished from the "adjustment Home" which is described later.

Number of establishments, location and cost

In 1963 there were about 800 local authority Homes in England and

Wales, each for fewer than thirteen children. The majority of these were family group Homes, but some of them were adjustment Homes. The official census of children's Homes does not differentiate between the two. Family Homes are most likely to be found on housing estates in towns. Estimated unit cost £8 in 1962/63.

Refs. See bibliography: 16, paras. 478, 485; 19, paras. 45-50; 24, pp. 55-61.

THE PERMANENT SUBSTITUTE FAMILY IN A PUBLICLY OWNED BUILDING

Description

Four-bedroomed council houses, exactly similar in design to other houses in private occupation, are rented by the County Council from the local housing authority. Two extra wash-basins are installed. There is no separate sitting-room for the staff. The County Council gives the couple in charge an annual allowance of about £350 allocated under various headings—for example, £135 for clothing and £10 for internal decoration. In addition the Council pays the rent and rates and the food bills. The houseparents submit accounts for their expenditure to the Council.

Purpose

The intention is to provide a permanent substitute family for children in respect of whom there is little or no hope that they will return to the care of their own families, without entailing the risks inherent in boarding out in private families.

History

Several of these Homes have been opened by the West Sussex County Council since 1955. It is not known that they have been copied anywhere else.

Number of children, age and sex

There are never more than six children in addition to the couple's own sons and daughters. Children are not generally admitted younger than five, but they stay to any age, until they marry or leave home to work at a distance. Exceptionally, a child may return to his relatives or be boarded out with someone with whom he already has a close contact. All Homes are of mixed sex. The Homes contain many groups of real brothers and sisters.

F

Staff

Living in the Home are a married couple, the wife alone being a paid employee. Her husband is able to follow his own employment outside the Home: he is expected to contribute £50 a year towards the cost of his board and lodging. If the husband dies, the widow may be invited to continue in the post on her own. A half-time non-resident domestic is paid for by the Council, and she may come in for an evening occasionally to allow the couple to have a night out.

Special features

This experiment has proved exceptionally successful with children who are not in touch with their own parents. The children are told they can stay until they are grown up and that they will not be boarded out or required to leave the home on reaching adulthood except at their own wish. The houseparents undertake to stay indefinitely. They like this arrangement and several couples have been looking after their groups of children for nine years and appear likely to remain. They have the minimum of official visitation, and one child care officer (professional caseworker) is attached to each Home to maintain the link with the County Council. Even the Children's Officer (Head of Children's Department) does not visit more than three times a year. The couple do not expect to take holidays separately from the children or to have official off-duty periods, the housemother being satisfied with the free time she gets when the children are at day school. A difficulty which has not yet arisen, but which must arise in future, is what to do when the couple are getting too old to go on rearing children so that no more children can be introduced as the older ones leave home.

Number of establishments, location and cost

The West Sussex County Council have nine of these Homes at present and more are being built. The majority of them are situated in new towns (towns which have been enlarged systematically since the war to take the overspill from London). Unit cost £6 4s. 0d. in 1964.

Refs. See bibliography: *1*, pp. 4 and 5; *28*, p. 3; *29*, p. 7.

THE LARGER SINGLE HOME

Description

The larger single Home occupies a position midway between the "family group" Home and the grouped Home. It is generally adapted from a large private dwelling-house though there have been in the past a number of purposely built establishments. Very large purposely built Homes, now disparagingly referred to as "barrack Homes", have fallen into disfavour and most of them have been closed.

Purpose

This type of Home is still used by some local authorities for short-term and long-term care, and it finds widespread favour amongst voluntary societies. Many of the smaller voluntary children's societies have as their principal purpose the maintenance of one or two Homes of this type for the long-term care of children entrusted to them by their relatives.

History

Large single Homes were first set up by poor law authorities and voluntary societies in the late nineteenth century, when the care of children first began to be differentiated from that of other poor people in the General Mixed Workhouse. Some agencies went on to develop Scattered Homes and others Grouped Homes, but the large Single Home has never entirely gone out of favour. Some authorities are now reverting to the use of these Homes following unhappy experiences in the management of "family group" Homes.

Number of children, age and sex

These Homes are used primarily for schoolchildren though, exceptionally, there may be a few occupants who are under or over school age. The minimum number of children is thirteen and there is no upper limit, though Homes exceeding fifty children are rare and the average is about twenty. Most of them are for boys and girls together, but a number are restricted to one sex.

Staff

It is usual to have a married couple in charge, especially when the Home population includes older boys. There will be assistant house-mothers (and occasionally housefathers) bringing the total resident staff up to a ratio of about one to five children, with non-resident cooks and domestics. Some of the resident staff hold the Home Office Certificate in Residential Child Care and Matrons are sometimes recruited from state registered nurses.

Special features

(i) It is easier to staff a Home of this type than almost any other establishment mentioned in this book. The majority of the children are assumed not to present exceptionally difficult behaviour. The staff are not thrown into each other's company to the same extent as in smaller houses, and it is much easier to arrange leave and time off.

(ii) It is claimed that in the less intimate personal relationships of a larger group the children are not subjected to the same degrees of stress. There is more opportunity for selection in forming relationships. The child is able to choose his special friends, and there are more members of the staff from amongst whom he can find one or more with whom he can form a relatively close tie. Against this it may be argued that the child gets less individual attention from the grown-ups and that the risk of "institutionalisation" is enhanced.

Number of establishments, location and cost

In 1963 there were about 1,000 local authority Homes and about 500 voluntary Societies' Homes, each for more than twelve children. They are to be found in all settings, both urban and rural. Estimated unit cost £8 in 1962/63.

Refs. See bibliography: *14*; *16*, paras. 157-271.

THE GROUPED HOME

Description and purpose

Grouped Cottage Homes are specially built by local authorities and voluntary societies, in the form of half a dozen or more detached or semi-detached houses on a campus, for the accommodation of children in their care. The intention is to combine the advantage of continuous care by the same adults in a small group with the benefit of the common facilities and services which can be provided economically for a large group. Grouped Cottage Homes generally have their own playing-fields, assembly halls, sick bays and central stores, and some have additional facilities such as chapels and swimming baths. Each group generally has a superintendent living in a separate house on the site with an office from which he administers the whole group with varying degrees of responsibility devolved to the person in charge of each cottage.

History

The first grouped cottages, or "Children's Villages", in England were built by Dr. Barnardo in the last quarter of the nineteenth century. This initiative was followed by Dr. Stephenson for the National

Children's Home and, in the early twentieth century, by many Public Authorities. The last to be built was completed shortly before the Second World War, by which time nearly half the children in public care were in grouped Homes. During the first half of this century opinion was divided between the merits of "Grouped Homes" and "Scattered Homes", the latter being set out amongst the ordinary streets of a town and administered by a superintendent living locally. The Curtis Committee, reporting in 1946, made no recommendation for or against the continuance of Grouped Homes, but advocated experiment with, and development of, small family group Homes which would be run autonomously by the person in charge of each Home under the general direction of the chief officer of the children's committee or voluntary society. In addition to the cottages for school-age children there were often special nursery buildings for children under school age, a receiving Home for newly admitted children and a hostel for those who had left school. At first the emphasis was on economising by rigorous centralisation—the food being cooked in a central kitchen and either served in the main dining hall or distributed ready-cooked for consumption in the cottages. Similarly, there were sometimes special schools on the premises, attended exclusively by the children from the Homes. Since the Second World War (and in many instances even earlier) there has been a marked trend away from excessive centralisation, and there are now few, if any, Grouped Homes where the children do not go out to ordinary schools and have meals cooked in their own cottages. The trend in local authority care has been very strongly against the Grouped Home. Many have been closed since the war and other closures are planned. Two large voluntary societies have, however, retained but refined their methods of care in Grouped Homes, by adapting the premises and reducing the size of each group.

Number of children, age and sex

Almost invariably, there are both boys and girls in a group of Homes. At first it was usual to put boys and girls into separate cottages, but the majority of cottages now contain mixed groups. Some authorities find that they have a high preponderance of boys in residential care, and then some of the cottages have to be used exclusively for boys. It was also usual to keep children in Nurseries until they reached school age and then to transfer them to the cottages, but it is becoming increasingly common for children under five to live in the cottages. The number of children in a single cottage may vary from six to twenty and the total of children in a group from fifty to three hundred.

Staff

The superintendent may be a man (whose wife may or may not be matron). Less often the superintendent may be a single woman. In the larger groups there will be a deputy superintendent. The cottages may be staffed in the same way as family group Homes with a married woman in charge, her husband going out daily from the cottage to work, either as a clerk, handyman or gardener on the estate or else in some occupation dissociated from the Grouped Homes. If each cottage contains more than a dozen children it will have an assistant housemother. There may be one or more relief housemothers to take charge of a cottage during off-duty time, sickness and annual leave, or there may be arrangements by which neighbouring cottages are paired, the staff relieving each other.

Special features

(i) In former times the régime in Grouped Homes differed substantially from that in Scattered Homes. A great many activities were centred on the group: it had its own church, its own Scout and Guide and other clubs, its own football team. Children were dissuaded from going outside the campus, or even forbidden to do so. The groups were closed communities, modelled on the boarding schools of the affluent. The modern tendency is to encourage the children to mix as much as possible with children living outside in their own families, although it is exceedingly difficult to arrange this effectively.

(ii) The tide of opinion flowed fiercely against Grouped Homes amongst those appointed in 1948 as officers of local authority children's committees. Nearly all the groups are likely to close in the fairly near future. The disadvantages of the Grouped Home are obvious: the child is brought up in an artifical child-centred community, the effects of which are only partially alleviated by sending him outside for school and play. Outside he again finds himself in the company of other children from the group. The close central control dissuades married couples of initiative from applying to join the staff as houseparents. Experience of the alternative family group Homes has, however, shown that these, too, have serious disadvantages of a different kind. This experience has caused some observers to look again at the compensating advantages of the groups. These are that, so long as there are any single women coming forward to run the cottages, the system facilitates their recruitment and retention in a community of like-minded people enjoying the support and leadership of a superintendent who takes the ultimate responsibility. Crises are not faced unsupported as they are in isolated Homes. The children directly benefit from having a larger choice of adults in the group to whom to relate. If a house-mother leaves an isolated Home the children start entirely afresh: in a Grouped Home the senior staff and many others on the campus remain even when a housemother leaves.

(iii) The successful cottage mother in a Grouped Home is a different kind of person from her counterpart in a Scattered Home. It may be that the grouped system is particularly suitable for Homes run by religious societies, where the corporate life is founded upon a common Faith. Nevertheless, since it is probable that the supply of young unmarried women will fail to equal the need in the foreseeable future it is unlikely that local authorities will alter their plans for the closure of Grouped Homes.

Number of establishments, location and cost

There are perhaps a dozen Grouped Homes run by voluntary societies and a larger number of Grouped Homes run by local authorities. The majority are located in small towns or on the outskirts of big cities. There are no published figures of average cost and these are difficult to estimate because the buildings, having been erected so long ago, are free of mortgage charges and because many administrative services are provided in Grouped Cottages which in the case of Scattered Homes are provided by the central organisation and not charged to the Homes. It seems likely that the cost of bringing children up in Grouped Homes is less than in Scattered Homes. It is worth noting, however, that the chairman of a very large authority, with great experience of both, has emphatically expressed the contrary view. There are no reliable estimates of unit costs.

Ref. See bibliography: *16*, paras. 476-96.

THE HOSTEL FOR WORKING BOYS AND GIRLS

Description and purpose

The statutory term "Hostels" (as opposed to Probation Hostels and Hostels for maladjusted children) is taken from S. 19 of the Children Act, 1948, which empowers local authorities to provide hostels for children in care who are over compulsory school age and for others who are over eighteen and under twenty-one. In contrast with current thought concerning most other residential establishments, it is felt to be positively desirable not to have a purposely built house, but to adapt a large dwelling-house. Such houses are thought to be less institutional in appearance and to make the residents and their associates less conscious of the fact that it is not an ordinary house. The acknowledged purpose of hostels was at first exclusively to accommodate young people who were either working or seeking work or else receiving education or training. This excluded, for example, young people who were psychiatrically disabled and for the time being unable to work, and expectant mothers whose pregnancy was too far advanced for them to work, but their scope was extended by an Act of Parliament in 1963.

History

Local authorities and voluntary societies have been running hostels since before the War of 1914-18. Poor law guardians not uncommonly used one of their scattered or grouped cottage Homes into which to transfer children when they reached school-leaving age. The provision of hostels for working boys and girls (both those formerly in their care and those who moved from their own homes to be near their work places) has attracted the interest of charitable societies for many years. In addition, for at least a century big employers boosted their labour force by providing hostels for some of their employees: naturally these hostels were most frequently used by the youngest workers.

Rising costs and the reaction against paternal employers have closed many of the firms' hostels. The drive for boarding out has meant that most of the young people remaining in local authority and voluntary hostels are those whose behaviour is such as to make them unacceptable as lodgers or foster children in private houses.

Number of children, age and sex

There are some large hostels for boys with up to 100 beds in some of the larger cities and many of these cater for a transient population as well as for regular boarders. Local authority hostels tend to have from eight to twenty places, the girls' hostels tending to be rather smaller than the boys'. Whereas voluntary hostels generally have no age limit, the majority of young people in statutory hostels are between fifteen and eighteen. It is not generally found practicable to mix young people over eighteen with those who have just left school. They are practically all exclusively for one sex or the other, but there is at least one local authority mixed hostel and it is planned to open others.

Staff

The persons in charge of girls' hostels are generally single women. The boys' hostels may have a man or a married couple. The provision of assistants is generally on a restricted scale, partly because of the difficulty of getting suitable candidates for the job, partly because of the belief that young adults ought to be learning to take care of themselves and partly because the sort of person who makes an adequate deputy warden or deputy matron is likely, after a short period spent in gaining experience, to seek a post in charge. It is not uncommon to find hostels staffed by one person as warden or matron, asssisted by a succession of students or of persons who do not stay long. Girl's hostels may be staffed by two women friends. Cooks and cleaners will probably be non-resident.

Special features

(i) Hostels are intended to provide a clean and modestly comfortable home for young people who would otherwise be living in lodgings. They vary in régime according to the qualities and interests of the people in charge and the characteristics of the residents. Some wardens introduce a measure of self-government, and all hostels make provision for group activities in varying degree—the larger the hostel the more likely is it to provide a wide range of recreational facilities. There will also be some encouragement for the residents to widen their interests outside the hostel in preparation for leaving. There may be some simple corporate religious observances, talks and discussion groups to enhance fitness for adult life, vocational advice, and a measure of control over the spending of wages, particularly to ensure that a fair proportion is contributed towards board and lodging. Order and discipline are maintained by the personal influence of the staff and the group pressure of the residents with the ultimate sanction of expulsion from the hostel. This latter is ineffective for boys and girls in care, since they know the agency will then be obliged to find them somewhere else to live.

(ii) Many Hostels run by voluntary societies are able to provide a comfortable, inexpensive, ordered and stimulating environment for boys and girls from ordinary families, who would otherwise have to be living in expensive, and possibly lonely, lodgings. The local authority hostels and some voluntary hostels are different. Their clientele consists almost exclusively of young people whose habits and behaviour are so disordered as to make it impossible to maintain them in lodgings. Both types of establishment make a vital contribution to the child care service, and those catering for the more difficult enable many young people who might otherwise become social casualties—the potentially delinquent, promiscuous or unemployable—to grow through an especially disturbed phase of adolescence into a stage of relative maturity.

(iii) The Children Act enables local authorities to set up hostels which may provide for people up to the age of twenty-one; both those who have been in care and those who have not. The expense and the difficulty of finding suitable staff mean that the facilities are used almost exclusively for those to whom the authority owes a statutory duty; those who are in care and under the age of eighteen.

Number of establishments, location and cost

Voluntary hostels are so varied in type that a precise definition of a hostel would have to be formulated before a nation-wide census could be conducted. There are, however, about sixty local authority hostels in England and Wales, divided roughly equally between boys and girls. Their location is determined by the availability of work, and also to some extent by the paucity of suitable lodgings. They are therefore mainly in industrial towns. Unit cost £9 8s. 9d. in 1962/63, of which a proportion was met by the residents from their earnings.

Refs. See bibliography: *9*; *10*, para. 49.

CHAPTER FOURTEEN

ESTABLISHMENTS FOR CHILDREN WITH EXCEPTIONAL NEEDS

"THE ADJUSTMENT HOME"

Description and purpose

IN PHYSICAL STRUCTURE the adjustment Home is the same as for a family group Home (*q.v.*) It is generally purposely built or is adapted from a "council house".

The purpose of an adjustment Home is, however, entirely different from a family group Home. It is used for the relatively short-term care of children who show disturbances of behaviour, or whose attitude is such that it is considered inadvisable, for the time being, to place them in foster homes.

History

This type of Home has evolved from the family group Home because child-caring agencies have discovered that the more intimate attention which is given in a small group by understanding and patient houseparents often enables a child to get more insight into his situation and to adopt attitudes which enable him to be acceptable again in his own home or in a foster home. There is no literature on this topic, other than that relating generally to the care of maladjusted children.

Number of children, age and sex

Numbers vary from four up to eight. The children are mostly of school age, but there may be a few children who are below or above school age. The sexes are usually mixed, but it may be found advisable to care for very disturbed older children in a Home kept exclusively for one sex.

Staff

The adjustment Home needs a bigger staff than the family group Home. Whereas in the latter type of Home the staff go on holiday with the children and have time off together by arranging for someone to come in for one evening a week, in the former it is essential to have full-time professional staff on duty all the time and for them to have at least a day and a half off every week, and generous holidays away from the children. There must be three resident staff so that when one is away on holiday or sick leave it is still possible for the other two to have time off. This may be achieved by employing three single women or a married couple and a woman assistant. The husband and wife have to be ready to take some of their holidays and time off separately so as not to leave the assistant unsupported. They may be able to take an annual holiday together by temporarily employing an additional assistant or by arranging for most of the children to go elsewhere on holiday at the same time. There will also be some part-time domestic help.

Special features

(i) The adjustment Home may experience many of the difficulties of the family Home. In addition it has to cope with serious behaviour and disciplinary problems. These difficulties are made more acute by reason of the proximity of staff to children. The small group encourages the child to display his feelings in a way which he would be unlikely to do in a crowd. The staff live so close to the children that it is difficult for them to get away from stressful situations, except when they are out of the house altogether.

(ii) Adjustment Homes differ from hostels for maladjusted children in that they are run by the ordinary child-caring agencies and not under psychiatric direction. The child guidance services are, of course, available for treating children and advising staff in the same way as for children in their own homes.

(iii) Children may remain for a short period or a very long one, but it is usual for them to leave for home or foster home after two or three years.

Number of establishments, location and cost

In 1963 there were 5,884 children in local authority care in Homes for fewer than thirteen children. Assuming an average of 7 to 8 children to each Home there was a combined total of 800 family group Homes and adjustment Homes in England and Wales with, in addition, a relatively small number of small Homes run by voluntary societies. It is not possible to divide this number between family Homes and adjustment Homes, since few local authorities differentiate formally between the two types. The Homes are mostly in towns and many are on new housing estates. Estimated unit cost £12 in 1962/63.

THE LONG-STAY NURSERY

Purpose

The long-stay Nursery provides care for children under five who have not been placed in foster homes, either because a sufficient number of foster mothers have not been found or because the child is suffering from some medical condition which is thought to demand special nursing care.

Description, history, numbers of children and staff (See The Reception Nursery, p. 140)

The long-stay Nursery is not yet systematically differentiated from the Reception Nursery. If an Authority maintains a Nursery it will be used both for reception and long-stay, according to the need of the moment. An increasing number of Authorities are, however, finding foster homes for all their long-stay children under five. In consequence, their remaining Nurseries are used exclusively for newly received children.

Special features ·

The deleterious effect, for some children, of care in Nurseries is likely to be more marked if the children stay for long periods. This leads many practitioners to seek foster homes for young children.

Number of establishments, location and cost

In 1960 there were 166 residential Nurseries provided by local authorities and perhaps another forty by voluntary societies. Some long-stay Nurseries are in the country, remote from the districts they serve, on the assumption that, since the children stay a long time, there is less reason to keep them close to their own families and to the place where foster homes are most likely to be found. This militates, however, against restoration to the child's own family or placement in a foster home. Estimated unit cost £13 in 1962/63.

Refs. See bibliography: *10*, paras. 44 and 45; *13*; *15*; *22*; *24*, pp. 61-63.

THE APPROVED SCHOOL

The Approved Schools constitute the largest single group of residential establishments discussed in this section. Approved School children number nearly a fifth of the 50,000 children who are estimated to be in residential care. We cannot do justice to this immensely important service in a few paragraphs, and we do not in any case claim to be writing about the special problems of caring for delinquents. For the sake of completeness some mention is nevertheless made; for more detailed information the reader is referred to the publications listed at the end of this section.

Description

The schools vary greatly. Some were purposely built over a hundred years ago and more are being built at present. Others have been set up in premises acquired by purchasing existing boarding schools or very large dwelling-houses. A third group have been converted from grouped cottage Homes. All the schools hold a certificate of approval granted by the Secretary of State under S. 79 of the Children and Young Persons Act, 1933. The system of management is the same as for Classifying Approved Schools (q.v.).

Purpose

The schools are used exclusively for the care and training of children who have been specifically committed by the juvenile courts as having committed offences or having been found (i) beyond control, (ii) in need of care, protection or control or (iii) failing to attend school. The children are selected by the courts on the ground that they need to be removed from home and given a fairly long period of residential training. The main task of the schools is described by the Home Office Children's Department,[1] as "the readjustment and social re-education of the child in preparation for his return to the community. The aim is to base the process of rehabilitation on understanding of each child's personality, history, abilities and aptitudes and a knowledge of the family situation. This process calls for a stable environment in the schools, enabling remedial influences to be brought to bear and progressive training to be given; it requires contact with the home to be maintained, and after-care to be thoroughly prepared for and carried out." This process can be examined under the following headings: Education, Practical Training, Health, Religion, Recreation and Leisure, Social Training and Personal Casework.

History

Reformatory Schools (for delinquents) and Industrial Schools (for homeless children) were established in the mid-nineteenth century by philanthropic endeavour. They were soon recognised by law and

[1] See bibliography : *10,* para. 184.

granted a subvention from public funds for each child whom they accepted from the courts. Over the years these two types of school have been integrated into a single approved school service. There have been periods of expansion, for example during the War of 1939-45, and of recession, as in the years from 1950 to 1956 when twenty-eight schools were closed. The demand for places in schools has increased since 1956 and, following an incident at a senior boys' school in 1959, there was an enquiry into the approved school system, which prompted the Government to provide money for the improvement of buildings and staffing. New schools are being set up by local authorities, but the majority of schools remain under voluntary boards of managers who are not accountable to the electorate.

Number of children, age and sex

Boys' schools range in size from about forty to well over a hundred: girls' schools tend to be smaller, the smallest having about twenty girls. Senior schools take children who have reached school-leaving age, junior schools take children from about eleven years old who are likely to be released at or before reaching fifteen and intermediate schools admit children between thirteen and fifteen who are likely to remain in the school after reaching the school-leaving age. The maximum point to which a child can be kept in a school is the nineteenth birthday. There are no mixed approved schools.

Staff

Approved schools have become relatively well staffed in recent years. Heads are generally qualified teachers or social workers and the staffs include a high proportion of teachers, housemasters and instructors, who live in or near the school and take part in a wide range of activities outside the schoolroom and workshops. The pay is good and the deductions for residential emoluments are small, but the hours are long and the work is exceptionally demanding. In some girls' schools the total staff, including domestics, may exceed fifty per cent of the number of girls.

Special features

(i) The former concept of the approved school as a place in which a child who had learnt anti-social ways at home was re-educated, is giving way to the idea of a therapeutic community in which children whose emotional development has been distorted are helped to develop new kinds of relationship. Some psychological and psychiatric advice is being provided for the staff. The schools are in a state of transition, in which the change in the nature of their populations has sometimes out-stripped the recruitment of staff qualified to undertake the new tasks.

(ii) The principal defects of the system are the isolation of some schools from the rest of the education and child care services and the lack of continuous casework help for children and their families. This could be remedied by vesting the parental rights in approved school children in some authority, such as the probation committee or the children's committee, which would operate in the child's home and take responsibility for the child from the moment he left home until he was re-established in the community.

(iii) As well as being classified by age the schools are also diversified to cater for children with different needs. Some provide special teaching for dull children and others for the intellectually bright. The senior boys' schools have different types of instruction, with emphasis on such callings as farming, building and seafaring. A few schools provide psychiatric treatment. There are separate schools for Roman Catholics. There are no Jewish girls in approved schools and very few Jewish boys.

Number of establishments, location and cost

The following table shows the number of each type of school in England and Wales on 1st January, 1963:

	Boys	Girls	Total
Classifying	4	1	5
Senior	26	21	47
Intermediate	27	5	32
Junior	27	7	34
Total	84	34	118

The need for a measure of specialisation means that children from sparsely populated districts may be sent a long way from home. Many of the schools are set out in the country in places which are inaccessible by public transport. This does not seriously affect the staff and the attendant social workers who often have motor-cars, but it militates against visits from the children's families. Unit cost £15 1s. 9d. in 1963/64.

Refs. See bibliography: 5; 7; 10, paras. 168-213; 21.

THE HOSTEL FOR MALADJUSTED CHILDREN

Description and purpose

Hostels for maladjusted children differ from boarding schools for maladjusted children in that the children go out from hostels to the ordinary schools. Hostels were at one time regarded as providing a substitute for the child's own home, but they are increasingly becoming recognised as residential therapeutic groups which provide treatment for the child whilst parallel treatment is being provided for the parents by the child-guidance clinic with the aim that the child shall return home. Most hostels are set up in large dwelling-houses which have been adapted for the purpose. The majority are run by local education authorities and a few by voluntary societies. There are also a number of private children's Homes, run as commercial ventures, which take some maladjusted children from education authorities along with children placed privately by the parents: these cannot properly be described as hostels for maladjusted children, since there is generally only the most tenuous relationship with the child guidance clinic, or none at all.

History, number of children, age and sex

The first hostels were established during the War of 1939-45 to care for evacuated children whose behaviour was too difficult for them to live in private billets. The Education Act of 1944 empowered education authorities to provide hostels for any handicapped child and the power is now principally used for the handicap of maladjustment.

Most hostels accommodate between twelve and twenty children. The children may be of any age from five to sixteen—the majority falling into the group from ten to fifteen. It is usual to have girls and younger boys together and to have separate hostels for older boys.

Staff

Many hostels have a man and wife in charge, though some have a married or single man as warden with a single woman as matron. The work is specially demanding, and the ratio should be one staff member to three or four children, with domestic staff in addition. In selecting staff the primary consideration is personal suitability. Many staff members have no special training, but it is, of course, desirable to appoint persons with a qualification in teaching, psychology, social work or with the Residential Child Care Certificate.

Special features

(i) The régime is not dissimilar from that of a well-run children's Home but, since disturbed children are less able to find their own occupations happily, it is desirable to make specially generous provision for crafts, hobbies and activities. The smaller numbers and the outside schooling ensure that the child can choose from a variety of pursuits and the atmosphere can be more permissive and less regimented than in an approved school: it is even possible to allow a child to do nothing, if that is his choice for the time being.

(ii) The essential feature of treatment in a hostel for maladjusted children is that it is carried out under the direction, and with the help, of the team of workers in a child guidance clinic. Admission to the hostel will be on the recommendation of the medical director of a clinic and the child's special needs will be discussed with the hostel staff before he is accepted by them. Members of the clinic staff will visit the hostel regularly to discuss with the staff each child's progress and special difficulties. There may also be a visiting psycho-therapist who will have individual sessions with those children most likely to benefit from this kind of treatment. The psychiatric social workers from the clinic will be in touch with the parents to prepare them for the child's return to them and to keep the child and hostel staff in touch with the child's home.

(iii) A special difficulty arises from the fact that many hostels are not staffed to provide continuous care. More than half the hostels close for at least part of the school holidays. Whilst most of the children will benefit from holidays at home, it will not always be in a child's interest to send him home at the particular time when it has been planned to close the hostel for staff holidays. The Underwood Committee said, "No hostel should ever be closed if it is in the best interests of any child that he should stay there, and this should be borne in mind in staffing hostels" (para. 269).

Number of establishments, location and cost

There are about fifty hostels for maladjusted children. Many are situated in the country, where property is cheaper, but the current tendency is to place them in small towns or on the outskirts of large ones. It is very important to place them within reach of a variety of day schools. Estimated unit cost £10 in 1962.

Ref. See bibliography: 6, Chapter IX.

THE TRAINING HOME

Description, purpose and history

Training Homes are provided almost exclusively by voluntary societies. These are generally societies of a religious nature, but many of their children are placed and paid for by local authorities. They are generally in large converted dwelling-houses. The régime is similar to that in a Probation Home (q.v.).

The intention of Training Homes is to provide a secure environment and wholesome influences for adolescent girls whose sexual attitudes and behaviour are such as to expose them to exceptional moral risks.

Training Homes had their beginnings in the mid-nineteenth century, and they have continued since that time to provide for the needs of girls who might otherwise be sent to approved schools or probation Homes.

Number of children, age and sex

Most Training Homes cater for from twenty to forty girls between the ages of fifteen and seventeen. A girl may remain voluntarily after the eighteenth birthday, but since local authorities have no parental rights after that age they cannot compel a girl to remain. The expression "Training Home" is used exclusively for establishments for girls. There are, however, a few training establishments for boys, such as sea training schools and the unique community in Oxfordshire called Turners Court.

Staff

Many Training Homes are staffed by members of religious communities—Anglican and Roman Catholic nuns and officers of the Church Army and of the Salvation Army. Others are run by moral welfare workers who have been trained for social work. The ratio of staff to children may be one to ten. The domestic work of the Home is done by the girls themselves as part of their training.

Number of establishments, location and cost

There are about thirty-five training Homes in England and Wales. Most of them are situated in towns and cities near to heavy concentrations of population. There are no reliable estimates of unit cost, but this is exceptionally low because the staff willingly accept low salaries or, in the case of religious orders, receive none. One recently opened

Home is, however, charging local authorities 12 guineas a week for each girl.

There is no literature specifically on this topic.

THE PROBATION HOSTEL

Purpose

Probation Hostels are provided for young people over school-leaving age who have been found guilty of an offence or who are beyond control or in need of care, protection or control; and who are thought not to need institutional training in an approved school but who are nevertheless unlikely to maintain and control themselves in their own homes or in lodgings.

History

In 1914 Courts were empowered to put offenders on probation with a condition that they should reside in a particular place. In 1928 the Government agreed to contribute to the cost of maintaining such probationers in hostels. In the 1930's a number of special probation hostels were set up by voluntary societies. By S. 46 of the Criminal Justice Act, 1948, the establishment of a Probation Hostel and the appointment of the person in charge require the approval of the Home Secretary. Since then the central government and local authorities have increased their financial support and ninety-nine per cent of this cost is now met from the residents' contributions and public funds.

Number of children, age and sex

Probation Hostels are provided for girls and boys separately; there are no mixed ones. The age range is from fifteen to twenty-one, but each hostel caters for a three- or four-year span within this range— say fifteen to eighteen, or seventeen to twenty-one. Numbers range from twelve to thirty, most hostels having between eighteen and twenty-five places.

Staff

Boys' hostels have a warden and matron, generally a married couple. Girls' hostels have a matron. There are also assistant supervisors of the same sex as the residents, bringing the ratio to about one member of staff to five residents, with cooks and domestic staff in addition. Very few persons working in hostels have any prior training, as distinct from experience, and they are not so well paid as persons with comparable responsibilities in approved schools and remand homes.

Special features

(i) Residents are expected to start going out to work within six weeks of coming to live in the hostel, and their wages go towards the cost of their maintenance, after which they receive back a standard amount of pocket money. There is more restriction than in an ordinary hostel, discipline being maintained by the personal influence of the staff with the sanction of reappearance in court for committal to an approved school. Domestic standards are wholesome, without providing amenities which the residents could not hope to enjoy when they leave. Facilities for recreation are provided, but residents are encouraged to learn to use some of their leisure for activities outside. Corporal punishment is prohibited. The length of stay is generally between six and twelve months.

(ii) Social casework is provided by co-operation between the probation officer of the committing court and the staff of the hostel, with the assistance of a "liaison probation officer" specially appointed in the district where the hostel is situated. There is no specialization, except as to age and sex. A survey is one area in 1954-6 showed that nearly half the boys admitted to hostels had no further serious convictions within two years of leaving the hostel.

Number of establishments, location and cost

In 1962 there were twenty hostels for boys and twelve for girls, providing 400 and 250 places respectively. The hostels were mostly situated in large cities. Unit cost £8 10s. 0d. in 1960, of which a proportion was met by the residents from their earnings.

Ref. See bibliography: *18*.

THE PROBATION HOME

Purpose

Probation Homes are similar in purpose and description to Probation Hostels. The important difference is that young people in Probation Hostels go out to work, whereas those in Probation Homes are occupied entirely within the Home throughout their stay. This makes the Home also similar in purpose to a short-term Approved School. It differs from the Approved School in that it is not so well staffed and equipped and that the residents are not under legal detention and cannot be compelled to remain there or to return after absconding (although they are, in some cases, subject to the sanction of being taken back to court for an approved school order).

History

The administrative history of Probation Homes is identical with that of Probation Hostels. The setting up of Probation Homes proceeded rather more rapidly in the early years. As early as 1923 over 500 young people were committed to Homes in twelve months.

Number of children, age and sex

Probation Homes are provided for boys and girls separately: there are no mixed ones. The age range is from fifteen to twenty-one and the tendency is for each Home to specialise in a more limited age range. There is only one Home for fewer than twenty residents and there are only two for more than thirty.

Staff

Staffing in general is similar to that in Probation Hostels, but there is greater emphasis on the need for occupation and training, since the residents do not go out to work. The supervisory staff ratio may therefore be higher and the domestic staff ratio considerably lower.

Special features

(i) The régime in Probation Homes is designed to help the young person who needs to be protected for a time from the temptations to which he would be subject in the community and to be given a short course of re-education in wholesome domestic and industrial habits. It is said to carry less social stigma than a term in an Approved School and is perhaps most suitable for girls displaying disordered sexual behaviour, who are expected to reach a more mature stage of development within a short time. The training consists largely of farming, gardening and woodwork for boys and domestic work for girls. Leisure time is largely occupied within the Home, boys being encouraged to spend some of their time outside the Home to a greater extent than girls. Corporal punishment is prohibited.

(ii) Liaison with the Probation casework service is identical with that for Probation Hostels. There is said to be an objection in principle to Probation Homes, since Probation is supposed to be restricted to "treatment in the open". A government committee reporting in 1960 said that it should be possible to provide satisfactorily in short-term Approved Schools and Probation Hostels for persons now sent to Probation Homes, provided the persons within the Approved Schools were cared for in small groups. The special value of the Probation

Home is that it is possible to relate the length of detention more closely to the needs of the individual resident. The special difficulty lies in giving an adequate and varied training in a small group with very limited staff and facilities.

Number of establishments, location and cost

In 1960 there were 4 Homes for boys and seven for girls, providing 120 and 160 places respectively. Since there is no need to be within reach of daily employment, some of the Homes are situated outside the large cities. Estimated unit cost, £8 10s. 0d. in 1960.

Ref. See bibliography: *17*, paras. 510-30.

BIBLIOGRAPHY

*References in Part II of the book refer to numbered items
in Part II of this bibliography*

I

CHILD STUDY

Ainsworth, Mary, *et al. Deprivation of Maternal Care; A Reassessment of Its Effects*. Geneva: World Health Organisation, 1962.

Balint, Alice. *The Early Years of Life*. New York: Basic Books, 1954.

Bowlby, John. *Maternal Care and Mental Health*. Geneva: World Health Organisation, 1952.

Chesters, Gwendolen. *The Mothering of Young Children*. London: Faber and Faber, 1943.

Freud, Anna. *Psychoanalysis for Teachers and Parents*. New York: Emerson Books, 1935.

—— The Psychoanalytic Study of Infantile Feeding Disturbances. *The Psychoanalytic Study of the Child*, Vol. II. New York: International Universities Press, 1946.

Freud, Anna, and Burlingham, Dorothy. *Infants without Families*. New York: International Universities Press, 1944.

Ruben, Margarete. *Parent Guidance in the Nursery School*. New York: International Universities Press, 1960.

Robertson, James. *Young Children in Hospital*. London: Tavistock Publications, 1958. New York: Basic Books, 1959.

—— *Hospitals and Children—A Parent's-Eye View*. London: Gollancz, 1962. New York: International Universities Press, 1963.

Spitz, Rene. Hospitalism—an Inquiry into the Genesis of Psychiatric Conditions in Early Childhood. *Psychoanalytic Study of the Child*, Vols. II and III. New York: International Universities Press, 1960.

Thomas, Ruth. *Habit Training, Further Trying Habits, Children Who Dislike their Food, Temper Tantrums, Children's Fears, Fears and Jealousies*. London: National Association for Mental Health, Parent Guidance Series, 1947.

II

RESIDENTIAL CARE

1. Association of Children's Officers. *Bulletin No. 110.* Exeter: Association of Children's Officers, 1962.
2. Association of Headmasters, Headmistresses and Matrons of Approved Schools. *Approved Schools and the Future; Monograph No. 7.* Knutsford, Cheshire: Association of Headmasters, etc., 1955.
3. Burmeister, Eva. *The Professional Houseparent.* New York: Columbia University Press, 1960.
4. Caldicott Community. *Interim Report of the Children's Reception Centre.* Mersham, Kent: Caldicott Community, Ltd., 1959.
5. Durand, V. *Disturbances at Carlton Approved School. Cmnd. 937.* London: H.M.S.O., 1960.
6. Education, Ministry of. *Report of the Committee on Maladjusted Children ("The Underwood Committee").* London: H.M.S.O., 1955.
7. Gittins, John. *Approved School Boys.* London: H.M.S.O., 1955 (O.P.)
8. Hall, M. Penelope, and Howes, Ismene V. *Moral Welfare Work Undertaken by the Church of England.* London: Board for Social Responsibility of the Church of England. (Awaiting publication).
9. Home Office. *Children in Care in England and Wales. March, 1963. Cmnd. 2240.* London: H.M.S.O., 1963.
10. Home Office. *Eighth Report of the Work of the Children's Department.* London: H.M.S.O., 1961.
11. Home Office. *Memorandum on Approved School After Care.* London: H.M.S.O., 1955.
12. Home Office. *Memorandum on Reception Centres.* London: H.M.S.O., 1951.
13. Home Office. *Memorandum on the Care of Children under Five Years of Age.* London: H.M.S.O., 1955.
14. Home Office. *Memorandum on the Conduct of Children's Homes.* London: H.M.S.O., 1951.
15. Home Office. *Memorandum on the Provision and Conduct of Residential Nurseries.* London: H.M.S.O., 1950.
16. Home Office. *Report of the Care of Children Committee ("The Curtis Report"). Cmnd. 6922.* London: H.M.S.O., 1946.
17. Home Office. *Report of the Committee on Children and Young*

Persons ("*The Ingleby Committee*"). *Cmnd. 1191.* London: H.M.S.O., 1960.

18. Home Office. *Second Report of the Departmental Committee on the Probation Service ("The Morison Report"). Cmnd. 1800.* London: H.M.S.O., 1962.

19. Home Office. *Seventh Report of the Work of the Children's Department.* London: H.M.S.O., 1955.

20. Home Office. *Sixth Report of the Work of the Children's Department.* London: H.M.S.O., 1951.

21. Home Office. *Statistics relating to Approved Schools, Remand Homes and Detention Centres for 1962.* London: H.M.S.O., 1964.

22. Home Office. *The Needs of Young Children in Care.* London: H.M.S.O., 1964.

23. Institute of Municipal Treasurers, etc. *Children's Services Statistics, 1962-63.* London: Institute of Municipal Treasurers and Society of County Treasurers, 1963.

24. Liverpool City Council. *Then and Now—Report on the Work, Organisation and Development of the Liverpool Children's Department, 1949-63.* Liverpool: City Council, 1963.

25. Mayer, Morris F. *A Guide for Child Care Workers.* New York: Child Welfare League of America, 1958.

26. Mazzocchi, Elda Scarzella. *A Social Welfare Group in Milan.* Milan Stampato nella Tip. Edit. Libr. L. di G. Pirola, 1951.

27. Thomas, Ruth. *Children without Homes.* London: National Association for Mental Health, 1946 (O.P.).

28. West Sussex Children's Officer. *Annual Report for 1954-55.* Chichester: West Sussex County Council, 1955.

29. West Sussex Children's Officer. *Annual Report for 1957-58.* Chichester: West Sussex County Council, 1958.

30. Home Office. *Report on the Work of the Children's Department.* H.C. 155. London: H.M.S.O., 1964.

III

FILMS

Appel, Genevieve, and Aubry, Jenny. *Maternal Deprivation in Young Children.* 16 mm. Sound. English. Black and white. Running time 30 minutes. London: Tavistock Child Development Research Unit, W.1, 1953.

Church of England Children's Society. *Broken Home*. 16 mm. Sound. English. Black and white. Running time 22 minutes. London: Church of England Children's Society, S.E.11, 1962.

Doctor Barnardo's Homes. *Great Endeavours*. 16 mm. Sound. English. Black and white. Running time 22 minutes. London: Dr. Barnardo's Homes, E.1, 1959.

Doctor Barnardo's Homes. *Is this Your Life?* 16 mm. Sound. English. Black and white. Running time 16 minutes. London. Dr. Barnardo's Homes, E.1, 1962.

Doctor Barnardo's Homes. *Towards Happiness*. 16 mm. Sound. English. Colour. Running time 23 minutes. London: Dr. Barnardo's Homes, E.1, 1960.

Doctor Barnardo's Homes. *The Way Ahead*. 16 mm. Sound. English. Colour. Running time 18 minutes. London: Dr. Barnardo's Homes, E.1, 1963.

Home Office. *A Family Affair*. U.K. 1264. 16 mm. Sound. English. Black and white. Running time 17 minutes. London: Central Film Library, W.3., 1951.

Home Office. *A Sense of Belonging*. U.K. 1703. 16 mm. Sound. English. Black and white. Running time 20 minutes. London: Central Film Library, W.3., 1962.

Invalid Children's Aid Association. *No Magic Cure*. 16 mm. Sound. English. Black and white. Running time 15 minutes. London: Invalid Children's Aid Association, W.8, 1963.

Jewish Child Care Association. *The Deep Well*. 16 mm. Sound. English. Black and white. Running time 37 minutes. New York: Child Welfare League of America, 17, 1957.

National Children's Home. *Of Such is the Kingdom*. 16 mm. Sound. English. Black and white. Running time 38 minutes. London: National Children's Home, N.4, 1955.

National Children's Home. *The Trust of a Child*. 16 mm. Sound. English. Black and white. Running time 38 minutes. London: National Children's Home, N.4, 1959.

National Children's Home. *Who Cares?* 16 mm. Sound. English. Colour. Running time 36 minutes. London: National Children's Home, N.4 1964.

Robertson, J. *A Two-Year-Old goes to Hospital*. Full-length scientific version. Sound. English or French. Black and white. Running time 45 minutes. London: Tavistock Child Development Research Unit, W.1, 1952. Abridged version. Running time 30 minutes, 1959.

Robertson, J. *Going to Hospital with Mother*. 16 mm. Sound. English or French. Black and white. Running time 40 minutes. London: Tavistock Child Development Research Unit, W.1, 1958.

Sailors' Children's Society. *A Family Affair*. 16 mm. Sound. English. Colour. Running time 30 minutes. Hull: Sailors' Children's Society, 1960.

Sailors' Children's Society. *One Hundred Years of Care*. 16 mm. Sound. English. Colour. Running time 20 minutes. Hull: Sailors' Children's Society, 1963.

Southwark Catholic Children's Society. *Safe in His Own Home*. 16 mm. Silent. Black and white. Running time 15 minutes. London: Southwark Catholic Children's Society, S.E.1, 1960.

Trieste Centro Cinematografia Sociale. *At least let me play*. C.263. 16 mm. Sound. English. Black and white. Running time 20 minutes. Geneva: United Nations Film Library. London: National Council of Social Service, W.C.1, 1961.

INDEX